# Bullied Back to Life

**How victims of bullying have used their experiences to fuel their success, and how you can too.**

Printed in the United Kingdom
First Printing, 2019

ISBN: 978-1-9162590-0-3 (Paperback)
ISBN: 978-1-9162590-1-0 (eBook)

Graham Harris
Loughborough, LE12 8WX

# Contents

# Dedication

**To the bullied and to bullies
– let's all find a way to stop this.**

# Introduction

When an object struck me on the chin as a young child, back in the infant school playground during break time one afternoon, it felt like someone had attacked me with a sledgehammer. The searing pain was immediate. I rocked on my heels, almost losing consciousness, like a boxer who had just taken a damaging uppercut to their jaw. I somehow jolted myself upright, as if to show whoever was responsible that it didn't hurt. I glanced down to see a smashed apple a few yards away. I then remember turning around full circle, probing for the 'hero' who threw the apple and instead noticed a sea of laughing faces. That reaction crushed my soul and continued to haunt me for many years.

Although I was in agonising pain, the thought of those children taking pleasure from my humiliation hurt me much more. I felt like I was a worthless lost child.

I didn't want to give those children the satisfaction of seeing my tears and used all my inner strength to hold them back, at least for a few more minutes. My chin was swelling up to almost double its size as I staggered towards the school building, struggling to retain the morsel of dignity I felt I had left in me. I wasn't heading in to tell a teacher – I know now I could or should have done. Instead, I made for an empty classroom where I calmly shut the door, trying not to attract any more attention to myself before sitting under a table to seek refuge. I cried my eyes out, sobbing in private, so I could keep a shred of my self-respect intact. I felt I wasn't even worth someone else's apple!

Looking back to that playground experience there are three types of behaviour that reflect the pattern of our world: **the bullied, the bullies, and the bystanders** (who choose not to help). However, the good news is, there's a fourth type.

I'd like to think that most of the children who witnessed what happened to me that day evolved into this fourth type!

So, what is this fourth type?

I became the fourth type, and the brave and wonderful people who have contributed their stories to this book are the fourth type too.

The fourth type are those who stand up to bullying to try and stamp it out when they see it happening.

They intervene, and in ways in which have humbled my heart, in ways different to each other, but all in ways that have helped to heal the hearts of the oppressed.

> **❝ Strong people stand up for ❞ themselves, but the strongest people stand up for others.**
>
> — Chris Gardner

Sharing their stories has already helped and encouraged many of these victims of violence and wrongdoing. It was the decision I chose to make too, in writing this book. Time, I thought, to come out of the shadows and tell my story and ask others to retell theirs so that we might all begin to open people up to the realities that surround us all in one form or another.

What do we all have in common, those of us who have retold our stories for the sake of this book?

Maybe, because of the way we have endured punishment, we have all developed a sixth sense, some invisible radar that picks out situations where acts of bullying are about to happen or are already in full flight. We stand alongside the bullied, in their corner, doing what we can in our own way, often quietly, yet effectively. You too can do the same after reading this book, if you're not doing so already!

Sometimes it takes being bullied for people such as the contributors of these chapters in my book to react in such a protective way. We can take some comfort from the fact that we have shared our experiences; we have stood up and made our message clear, because we see it as our duty and our calling!

Those who have agreed to write about their personal experiences have all been bullied, abused, belittled, humiliated and trampled on like dirt. The common denominator in all of us is that we see the good in the bad, the light in the darkness and share the hope that any of the three types of behavioural types can move to become the fourth. All the people included in the following chapters have achieved success in spite of such adversity. In many cases these are different versions of success, not always the one you might expect.

Bullied, bullies and bystanders can all step up and stand up to bullying. This can often be incredibly difficult, but we can all intercede when someone is singled out and made an outcast. I don't mean in a way that places us in physical danger. This book shows us how, no matter who we are, what we've done in the past or what burdens we carry, it's never too late to change our mindset.

Have you ever gone back in time to relive a difficult or traumatic phase in your life? I mean really travelled back to your most heart-breaking experience to painfully scan, with your older eyes and open heart, something that almost broke you in order to try and understand what the hell happened, and why?

If the answer is yes, you will know how agonising, depressing and upsetting it can be.

I have asked six people to go back in time, as older and wiser people, after I had revisited my own heart-breaking moments, to ensure that whoever read our vivid testimonies would feel our pain and learn from our experiences.

I asked each person, like me, to share what they felt at the time of that beating, that put-down demeaning comment or that continual tirade of mental aggression and torture. I then asked each of them to re-evaluate why they thought it had happened, whether they understood the reasons enough to forgive, or maybe there was no real reason to speak of. I asked how their experiences in being bullied affected their whole lives, right up to the present day, and how they have reached a point of becoming a positive and successful version of themselves.

It hasn't been easy, there have been some tears along the way. I've pushed and pushed for contributors to open up their wounds and pushed again for them to then go deeper. It is so important that we don't play down what happened and that our stories will encourage more books like this to be written. Not all of us as individuals answered every question. That's a tough ask considering the subject matter, but collectively I like to think we have covered them all.

Somehow, over the years, I managed to hide, block or deny my bad memories to forge my own version of success, because of or even in spite of what happened. So, it's been immensely comforting to find more individuals who have turned similar adversity into a positive driver. From this, I hope that others who haven't or can't reconcile their dark past might learn something from their stories too. The idea is to help to mend people's brokenness, the helplessness they still feel today.

This book had to be written, despite my reservations and concerns. Not many adults openly discuss anything associated with bullying. Even if you haven't been bullied, it's more than likely that you have witnessed an act of bullying or dare I say, either bullied or demonstrated at least an act of aggression towards someone else!

So, every one of us has, or knows someone who has, displayed one of those three types of behaviour:

# Bullied, bully or bystander

Not something we all voluntarily admit to, is it? If it all happened long ago, we bury or deny it, don't we?

That seems harsh, I know, but hear me out – I set out to stand up to the act of being bullied, but after researching bullying and finding out more, I have become more aware of how easy we can slip into behavioural patterns, particularly when under stress.

"Bullying", as described in Wikipedia, is "the use of coercion, force, or threat, to abuse, aggressively dominate or intimidate. The behaviour is often repeated and habitual. One essential prerequisite is the perception (by the bully or by others) of an imbalance of physical or social power. This imbalance distinguishes bullying from conflict."

And that is only the short definition; there's far more, so there's room for debate. The tag 'bully' sounds harsh and undesirable to me, and so I can't think of anyone who'd particularly want that label. Therefore, one of my goals is to help make readers self-aware of their own behaviour.

There are times when I've called the odds to get my point across, where my passion has got the better of me, and I am sure you might have done something similar. We can be passionate, and I think that is fine, but bullying is a whole different thing. The danger is that we can all so easily cross the line. It's not what we think that matters, it's what those on the receiving end of something we ourselves only perceive as strong emotion feels too.

> **❝ Courage is fire, and ❞ bullying is smoke.**
>
> — Benjamin Disraeli

Over the last few months I have become a volunteer for the amazing Cardiff charity, BulliesOut, and this is just one piece they included in their "Bullying hurts" leaflet:

"Bullying has no genre and is not part of growing up!

One incident of bullying behaviour is serious enough, but when it is persistent over a period of time it becomes a devastating problem. The detrimental impact bullying can have on the physical, emotional, academic, social and personal wellbeing of a person cannot be underestimated.

At best, bullying causes great distress which can continue right through adulthood. At worst, bullying can lead to self-harm and suicide..."

BulliesOut have also published a statement I couldn't agree with more...

"Bullying has long been clouded by a fog of silence and a 'culture of telling' needs to be created. Bullying is a very stressful ordeal – one that many people find it hard to speak about. However, children and young people, parents and professionals need to feel confident that if reported, bullying will be dealt with appropriately."

My hope is that through the stories and information in this book, you will find examples of true courage that will inspire you, regardless of what degree of adversity or suffering you may have personally encountered. There has to be a way for past victims of bullying to find some closure and make sense of what happened, enough to turn such terrible experiences into a positive force for others to learn from.

I sincerely hope, also, that the resources in this book will prompt those of you being bullied or who know of someone encountering bullying, to make that call for support. In this way we can all begin to make this crippling act of intimidation and power a thing of the past!

# Chapter 1

# The moment it all started

**I**n the school playground, aged 8, I snatched a skipping rope from Johnny Penner.

That's all it was.

That tiny, seemingly trivial incident, motivated by nothing more than an 8-year old's silliness, brought down on my head (and various other parts of my body...) a 6-month campaign of bullying that decades later is the trigger for this book.

I didn't even really want the skipping rope...

# Why I have written
# *Bullied Back to Life*

I had just finished reading through what should have been the final draft of my first ever book, *Against the Grain: How I went from factory floor to my own multi-million-pound company (and how you could too)*, but there was something missing and I just couldn't put my finger on it. The bullies were lurking...

Of course, I was proud that I had poured my heart and soul into typing out my amazing and quite surreal business adventure, that to this day I still have to pinch myself on a regular basis to know for sure it really happened.

That adventure included me starting out as a schoolboy with no qualifications, stumbling into being a factory floor no hoper, to eventually, at the grand old age of 36, setting up a global distribution channel to sell my very own patented products – how did that happen, no, why did it take so long for me to realise I was capable of making all that happen?

But my book, which I had needed to read myself to try and fathom how on God's earth it had all actually unfolded, was missing a key link, something personal from my past, a memory buried deep inside that was a significant part of what drove me to the success no one who knew me would ever have predicted.

Yeah, yeah, yeah, I'd spilled out of me the David v Goliath triumph stuff, the little guy made good, and I'd included what I felt made the shy guy shine. I had wanted to show my readers that anything is possible, no matter what barriers lie before us, but all along I knew I was avoiding my elephant in the room.

I so needed that book to reflect me, warts and all, but all the time careful not to portray myself misleadingly as some kind of hard-nosed stereotypical business person who'd trample over everyone in their path to claim their just reward.

I was so careful not to falsely portray myself as someone who used intimidation in any shape or form, but my self-inflicted therapy session was getting me closer to what my subconscious mind was probing for.

A deep scar was about to be opened; I could sense it. They're getting closer...

The near-empty glass of wine I was holding needed topping up, I was feeling anxious and rather emotional and it took a few more large gulps to bring what I was searching for to the surface.

You see, my then editor, Mark Eglinton, had pushed me to reveal to my readers what really makes a successful inventor tick, how they think, what are their character traits. I'd moved that from the general to the specific, laying bare what makes me tick and how I think.

My answers gave my book a depth and an honesty to it, but all the while I hadn't included everything!

It came to me – the intake of wine had helped to bring to the surface a painful memory I'd hidden for over 40 years.

**This was something that deep down I knew all along was the key motivator for my success – being bullied in the playground as a child.**

That was the elephant in the room – I'd just done my best to ignore it for too long.

In that moment of re-reading my book I could feel its huge weight again and I was overcome with feelings of hurt and sadness.

So there and then new words flowed out of my head and onto the laptop keyboard.

I started by tapping in the names of all those bullies, whose names I found I could recall perfectly. Then came the vivid details of what they put me through. This then all ended up in the first 3 pages of my book, *Against the Grain*.

## Reliving that moment

Two brothers, cousins to Johnny Penner, the boy whose skipping rope I'd grabbed in the playground, were looking for a new challenge, fresh meat, and right on cue I had presented it to them on a plate.

I'd upset their cousin and I would pay for my mistake, big time! They set about making my life a living hell.

I hadn't any idea of what was about to happen, my innocent mind could never have contemplated what I would go through.

As I remembered back to those painful events, it was as though it was happening all over again. As I was immediately reliving the first act of violence, I could still picture the face of the bully who'd pinned me down, his knees crushing my rib cage, his cold eyes piercing through my soul as he smashed my head into the pavement, not stopping at 3 or 4 strikes but a few more for good measure.

I remember thinking to myself, how could someone be capable of doing this, it made no sense, I just felt numb! It wasn't just blood that seeped out, it was my self-esteem and confidence that drained away too.

> **❝ I found one day in school a ❞ boy of medium size ill-treating a smaller boy. I expostulated, but he replied: 'The bigs hit me, so I hit the babies; that's fair.' In these words, he epitomized the history of the human race.**
>
> — Bertrand Russell

# What did I learn?

The brothers-in-arms, one who tortured me mentally and the other who beat me physically, began to recruit around 15 or so more boys and I was hunted down like a dog. Every break time and walks home after school consisted of me trying to defend myself from blindsided attacks and having to seek out new hiding places down alleys, behind cars or trees. Being cornered while 4 or 5 kids took it in turns to kick and punch me was part of my habitual ordeal. I remember one lad running up to kick me and I simply placed my foot in the air to block it. The sole of my shoe clashed with his shin and for once someone else was in agony.

That one move told me I just needed to outsmart some of the kids, even as the punishments rained down, day after day, week after week.

Delaying my walks to coincide with teachers' strolls home was a handy trick I learnt, and it served me well for a while, giving me temporary reprieve.

My young mind still couldn't comprehend how one boy, or a group of boys, could submit this kind of physical abuse on someone else. Years later, as a teenager, a school thug who saw me walking back from a football match, shouted out the location where some opposing fans were stranded on a piece of waste ground and asked if I would join him and his mates in the attack. I told him it wasn't my thing and he called me a coward. I remember glaring back and thinking to myself that he and his thuggish gang were the real cowards.

It also wasn't lost on me that this was how my bullies would have acted when I was the one stranded as an eight-year-old boy.

I had the most sunny-natured and kind-hearted mum I could ever wish for and I was blessed with possessing her kind nature too. Those cruel school time experiences nearly robbed me of that, but I held onto it, and all my other positive character traits as well. Those bullies weren't going to steal them away, no matter what they'd put me through.

Like most children who are physically bullied, I had asked myself, why me? That "why me" question turned into all sorts of other doubts: maybe I am different, undesirable, a misfit, one of those kids who always gets picked on, period. But even at that tender age I knew it was wrong and that I shouldn't submit to this easily, and I began to work out how to fight back.

Although I didn't know it back then, I now realise that I played my part in all this, being shy, naive and not at all street-wise. Simply put, I was sensitive and struggled to hide this part of me. This signalled to the bullies that I showed enough vulnerability for them to exploit to the full. My good nature was seen as an invitation for a good kicking.

So, was I subconsciously playing the part of the victim? Today I am still sensitive and feel vulnerable at times, but the difference is I now know how to use those feelings to my advantage.

I am proud of the fact that I've never felt guilty about having those characteristics as part of who I am. I was true to myself then and have continued to be all my life, not denying them because of what I went through then.

Back then I was tall for my age, a full head and shoulders above most of the boys of my age. I hadn't yet worked out how to fully control my limbs, you could say I was a bit like Bambi on ice, and this separated me from the rest and probably made me an even more likely target.

It made me smile recently when a friend of mine commented that it's hard to believe someone like me (being 6ft 4 as I stood before him) could have been bullied. I think he was judging me as he perceived me there and then, and besides from my book he wouldn't have known my full story. Maybe he'll begin to understand the full picture when he reads this book...

To master a certain skill, you learn how to overcome problems that challenge you. To master the act of being victimised and how it impacts on you personally, although it's sad, you yield to it. That's what I have learnt to do, and this book is testament to the fact that you don't need to feel guilty.

Out of weakness comes strength and out of strength comes the will to fight back. I'm not talking about physically fighting back, but more about the inner battle to win back your positivity, even after the experience appears to have left you.

But the battle often starts in a dark place, when victims of bullying are at their lowest and most vulnerable. This book is about the battle and how it can be fought and won.

## Learning from the experience

I don't want this book to define me as that business guy who harped on about being bullied and who played the victim, in the same way I don't want my first book to define me as an inventor or entrepreneur. That kind of stuff embarrasses me, but these subjects need to be explored whether I feel comfortable about them or not. Feeling comfortable would to me mean not addressing anything and just existing in safety, not using my experiences, good, bad or indifferent, to help anyone else.

I love writing about life experiences that matter. I want to express my feelings because they may reflect what many of you reading this feel too. We all have many facets to our character but not one alone needs to define us. Humans are fascinatingly multi-faceted and complex creatures, so let's keep the naysayers guessing.

Many people who see this book's title, *Bullied Back to Life*, before even opening it, may feel challenged or even threatened by what they think I am digging up.

Some will merely think that I should man up, take it on the chin (which I quite literally did) and let it go. Surely all is fair in love and war, what happened in the playground should stay in the playground, this stuff toughens us up.

Well, tell that to those whose lives have been destroyed, whose hopes and dreams have been quashed and whose futures have been stolen. Not all of us are so easily conditioned to handle aggression. Not everyone can easily come back from the dreadful feeling of being humiliated, victimised and having their identity crushed. For many of us who have yielded in the past to gross physical intimidation and mental cruelty, a lesson from this book is that you can be once bitten, twice shy. Being victimised, as testified in the stories in future chapters, can turn into a refusal to be victimised anymore, to learning how to cope by turning adversity on its head.

So, let's learn from some victims of bullying about how to move on and be stronger.

The boy who carried out my head smashing was the henchman for his brother. The brother never physically struck anyone throughout his schooling. Instead, he just used clever words to describe how he would take boys apart, including me, limb from limb. He was so convincing he controlled my mind for a while – that was the worst kind of intimidation. The mental cruelty I endured almost broke me, almost...

My world changed and from that moment it would never, ever be the same again. Yes, the intensity of the bullying subsided after 6 months, but the effects of it lived on. I'd just buried them! Quite regularly, as an older school child, teenager and young adult, those experiences found their way back into my life, often in ways I found I could handle much better, and sometimes in ways where I know I simply didn't. On those occasions I demonstrated a significant degree of physical retaliation. The learning curve left me with feelings of inner guilt, sadness and incredible insecurity, all of which you can read about in Chapter 2.

In my first book, the bullying episode was covered in just the first two-and-a-bit pages out of a 256-page book. In spite of just such a brief reference to it, it was the missing link needed to complete that book's story.

Some people close to me would have been shocked to learn of such adversity, and even my wife commented that it had opened up our previously well-guarded life to the world. Of course, she was right, but I had no regrets. I learnt through reliving my experiences that I wasn't weak and that they made me the person I am today. I wanted people to realise that this type of thing happens, and more commonly than most of us think.

For those of you who are experiencing the physical and/or mental effects of intimidation and bullying right now, this book will help you to find out how you can get through it, as well as offering you a list of resources and organisations which can help you.

When I was first attacked and beaten as a young child, my playground was my world, so in my innocent mind, my main tormentors were simply the biggest bullies in the whole world. I had no understanding that there were tens of thousands of other schools out there, which meant there were potentially thousands of other bullies wreaking havoc in other playgrounds.

I had no thoughts running through my brain that told me that my bullies would most definitely yield to most other bullies, in a similar way I yielded to them, if they were thrown into a pit with them. Small comfort now but take from this something positive, that you are not alone!

Bullies have big issues themselves – they are just cruelly transferring these onto you through cowardly behaviour and acts of violence. You are not the problem; they are the problem!

# How bullies operate

No one likes to be at the bottom of the pecking order in any given situation, but through experience I've learnt that some of us can handle it much better than others. The root cause of bullying is that bullies can't handle being anything below the top spot.

In my experience, there's always another pecking order where bullies can't maintain their status. When they inevitably become part of a new peer group, in a new school, location or workplace, they start off way back down the list. I learnt this when the bully who tried to control my mind got threatened by a boy from another school in the local park and had to grovel his way out of a fight. This gave me hope and the knowledge that there can be no absolute winners. We all need mending, bullies and bullied, so let's get started...

This book has been written against the advice of a few people pointing out that I am competing in a crowded genre. So what? "You won't make money from a book like that." I don't care about profiting from my book! What I do care about is helping people to use their bullying nightmares as positive motivation, like I did. And in fact, all proceeds from this book are being donated to the anti-bullying charity BulliesOut. See more info about BulliesOut in Chapter 10.

"So many inventors get it wrong, you should write about how, as a successful inventor, you can help them." No, I care more at this moment in time about helping to mend people's hearts and minds so they can unlock the chains that hold them prisoner. The inventor stuff can wait!

So, this is the book they told me not to write, the book I feel will open up wounds, challenge those who are tempted into intimidating others to think twice about doing it and help those who have been bullied to understand it's not them who have the problem.

And this is the book that I am most proud of, as the main aim is to help those victims of bullying to understand and come to terms with what is happening or has happened, so they can start to reach the potential they were put on this earth for. Isn't that the least we all deserve? That's what I did!

My feet are firmly rooted to the ground and I have no delusions of grandeur, I've simply made the most of what little talent I have possessed through using it quietly, patiently and diligently, without seeking anyone's opinion or permission. Through the tough times, I haven't given up or blamed something or someone from the past, I've simply taken responsibility for everything, as I believe that's the key to overcoming adversity.

It's an interesting question – what makes some people thrive and drive towards success after experiencing adversity?

I could answer this in many ways, but fundamentally, for me at least, it is coming to the realisation that if we don't do something about it, we usually end up living the life most people we know would want us to live, predict we would live, or feel comfortable with us living.

I really do think that our minds can easily be conditioned to play life safe, simply because we avoid the disappointment of potentially failing at something others may deem is above our station. We are in danger of staying within a peer group of similar people, not daring to discover what we are capable of doing.

I know so many people who have had more potential to succeed than me, and more talent, but they didn't/don't use it. So, one day, I made a decision to use my passion and the small ability I possessed to change my life, no matter what it would take. When I got my break, I pushed and pushed... and eventually became really good at it.

Someone once said to me (who knew about my seemingly modest back-story), "You have clearly punched way above your weight in terms of your business success". I just smiled back politely and thought to myself, no, you've just punched way below your weight, and settled for a safer life.

I haven't reached my full potential yet and if I am honest, I don't think I ever will. After all, who does? But what drives me to keep on the path of striving for it is being scared of going back to where I came from, to that playground, to the factory, to those places where I felt like a square peg in a round hole.

This may seem crazy to anyone reading this who hasn't been taunted and beaten physically... but as a victim, you can end up feeling that you deserve your punishment. When someone threw that apple in my face, as I described in my introduction, I thought I wasn't even worth someone's lunch!

I've had to battle my way back from that sad way of thinking. It has been a high mountain to climb, and I want to encourage those of you haunted by what has happened to you, or is still happening, to start that climb, one small step at a time.

I am a great believer that success isn't defined and measured by monetary gain or a collection of possessions we accumulate along the way. It's how we feel in our hearts, it's inner peace and an acceptance of ourselves that matters. I am conscious that for every person who reads this book whose life has been affected by some form of intimidation, that their intimidator most likely won't have turned a page and changed, so let's send them this book! Seriously, it's for them too – yes, I really think this book has great content to help those caught up in BOTH sides of this serious problem.

The bullying I had to endure might only be represented by a few paragraphs in the first chapter of my last book, one single entry in my life story that includes a wealth of experience in other areas, but it is the most important one in terms of how I have chosen to live my life: sink or swim, I chose to swim.

Regarding the bullying I have put up with and witnessed in others, I could have chosen a far safer life to ensure I didn't get hurt again, but bullies thrive in that type of situation, and I wasn't about to give them the satisfaction of owning my life, and you shouldn't either.

Without this sad aspect of my life I wouldn't have reached the heights I have ascended to in my business and in life. I will explain more about that later, but in thinking about this book I have realised that I need input from a wide range of people to understand this whole bullying issue. We'll be working it all out in considerable detail, from every angle, so that you'll be able to see things from a wide range of different perspectives. My story is my catalyst for writing this book, but it is just the start-point of the search for answers.

In this book you'll hear vivid personal testimonies from a number of people who have experienced various forms of bullying. Not only that, you'll find out how all of them have been able to use their bullying experiences to rebuild their lives and move forward.

**We will all learn together so that we are all bullied back to life.**

# Chapter 2

# How being bullied makes us feel and behave

I remember vividly how being bullied made me feel as an 8-year-old shy schoolboy, but I'd never really thought about how it might have made me behave, not only back then but during my adolescence and early 20s, until I needed to write about it. What I have dug up has disturbed me somewhat – it's like the penny has finally dropped, and frankly many times I have wished that I had let this all stay in the past.

But I'd have been doing myself a disservice and denied an opportunity of others benefiting from my story and those whose stories are also included in this book.

## Seeking acceptance

Probably the biggest realisation was how I must have come across to my peers and teachers as I sought validation and acceptance. Looking back now, I know I was most definitely rather irritating as I overcompensated my personality by trying really hard to impress, as a result of the rejection I had suffered.

The effects of bullying, I worked out, had made me feel as though I couldn't be loved, liked or thought of as normal, and this haunted me into my mid-20s, right up until when I married my wife.

It was only then, for the first time in years that I believed someone outside of my immediate family meant it when they said they loved me. My wife Sue started the healing process, although she never knew it. Her reading this sentence in this chapter will be the first time she finds out! I remember telling her, after only a couple of dates, that she will never know the real me. I think that was because I didn't even know who I truly was, what a jack-ass thing to say!

It is now so obvious to me all these years later why I wouldn't accept compliments until I'd found Sue and married her, and maybe struggled even beyond then – I'd constantly challenge any endearing remarks, whoever they came from, and throw them back.

## Bullying in business

The bullying in the playground did however prepare me for the intimidation, rejection and loneliness I would encounter and endure at the start of my inventor's journey almost 30 years later, and throughout the ups and downs of that bumpy ride.

It takes a monumental effort to bring an idea to the global market and then turn it into a successful product. Only a very small percentage of inventors manage to do this even once, let alone multiple times like I have. This demonstrates to me as much as anything that I haven't allowed bullying or any form of adversity I have met with to hold me back.

I have learnt that a significant proportion of the multiple rejections I have received when pitching my ideas or inventions to the industry giants in my sector have come about because of the perceived threat new technology brings to their "Gatekeepers." The Gatekeepers are usually the "Big Tech" guys who hold high positions in large companies because of what they have built up in terms of developing their organisation's existing solutions. They have the power to say yes or no to people like me who bring in something new that they may often see as a threat to their status. Sad and unfair, yes, but not personal!

Yes, I have had Gatekeepers try to intimidate me and reject my solutions, but it isn't me they hate, it is the idea of their security being threatened that they take a dislike to.

So, I have always refused to be bullied in these situations. I hold my head up high even though it usually doesn't change the outcome, and I move on with zero animosity. This has been the key to my success. No one can take away the belief and confidence I have in the technology I have invested in. I use this self-belief to navigate my way around such behaviour. And for sure, if I can do it, I believe anyone else can also begin to understand the psychology of what is really going on.

As a child, I realise now that I was ill-equipped to deal with what I interpreted as hatred and contempt towards me. Now, in adult life, I have made the decision to avoid completely any business people and organisations who bully and intimidate. I won't have people like that in my life! I am lucky enough now to have carved out a life where I can choose just to work with the good guys. Believe me, if you know how to look for them, there are plenty of good guys out there.

Is this a message for those who bullied me? No, it isn't. I don't care, that's all in the past and stays there. I care more about those of you reading this who can't let go of your past. I want you to know that you have a choice, that you deserve to aspire to achieve and experience what you desire. No one should be allowed to rob you of your dreams or have a negative impact on how your life unfolds years later.

Would I rather my bullying nightmare hadn't happened? If it would have been possible to change things back then, yes, I would have wished it away in a flash, but now? No, what I went through has made me the person I am today, someone who is stronger, tougher and more resilient because of it.

That doesn't mean I don't ever relive some bad stuff, feel incredibly vulnerable or suffer a few nightmares, but I've just somehow managed to park them away as soon as those flashbacks occur. I know I am fairly sensitive and often feel as though I still have something to prove to myself, but I honestly don't know if this is connected to my past. I've learnt to embrace these things because they drive me to my goals. I harness those bad experiences to fuel my determination. Besides, who doesn't feel like I sometimes feel?

**Even bullies feel vulnerable, that's one of the reasons they bully**

I've met and talked to several people who have experienced bullying in the past, and they can't let go, they cannot forget, and forgiving is not even on their radar. So, isn't it about time we all started to understand our own pain, and why another human being would want to intimidate us, so we can begin to mend what we may feel right now is irreparable?

It hasn't been easy to find victims of bullying willing to submit a story for this book. Some found it painful to rake up the past and others didn't want to risk someone connected to past events coming back into their lives, despite my assurances that the identities of bullies would be left out. A few who signed up initially later called me to drop out for some of those reasons and more. On every occasion I didn't apply any pressure or try to change their minds, as I totally understood – this is a terribly difficult thing to do.

Every person had a good reason to abstain. For example, one lady would have exposed potential miscarriages of justice and risked being put in grave danger all over again. Another had been virtually run out of town and needed to start all over again. In both instances I agreed that the risks were far too high.

However, I learnt so much from these two people and everyone else who simply couldn't contribute for a host of valid reasons, some of which have led to further research that supports this book. Thank you so much to all of you, I truly felt your pain and remain inspired by your positivity to win through your personal battles to find your own versions of success.

I did however note that all those who submitted something of their story felt strongly that they did it to try and help other victims whose suffering goes on, despite opening up their own personal wounds, and for this I am hugely indebted.

One contributor talked in detail about the shame of succumbing to the act of bullying. I really hope that he, along with all of you who continue to turn these pages, can begin to see that there really is no shame.

# How to fight back and how not to fight back

I'm now going to tell you about parts of my life which I haven't quite worked out yet. As you will see, these became, rightly or wrongly, ways for me to deal with the fact that I had succumbed to bullying and was now not going to yield to it again. These events happened many years prior to any thoughts of business success were conceived.

As an older schoolboy of about 14, my over-the-top comedic nature saw me attract trouble from what I can only describe as an intimidating boy two years older than me, with a reputation for doing damage to those he took a dislike too. Joking my way out of this one wasn't an option, but at least we were the same height.

I'd won three gold medals at judo, and I remember my instructor telling me only to use my fighting skills in self-defence, so that was my plan as the boy took his best shot, which I can still feel landing heavily in my face. Straightaway I managed to grab his other arm, pull him off balance and throw him clean over my shoulder.

That would have been a win on the judo mat, 10 points, but there was no walking away to exchange customary bows, so not knowing what to do I held him down on the ground and rained down a few rabbit punches, before asking if he would admit defeat if I let him go. Being rather naive and trustworthy, I released him after he agreed, and he then basically beat me up, dragging me across the playground, before him and a group of his friends all repeatedly spat on me as I lay defenceless.

That event at 14 was a humiliating and tough experience, but at least I'd not backed down. I had tried to stand up for myself, even if it had been a fat load of use.

I have retold that event many times since, and I have always added humour to it, as if I was describing a comedy sketch, and most definitely as though it happened to someone else. Maybe that is my coping mechanism.

## Making yourself a target

I remember getting into more scrapes through my over-exuberant way of portraying myself. I would hide my painfully shy nature by showing off, not realising until many years later that I had been playing into the hands of my more mature tormentors.

As a result, I ended up attracting the attention of more bullies. One in particular was known for his ability to administer a huge number of punches in a kind of windmill motion. Basically, we were all terrified of him, and when he approached me to set up a fight, I knew it was usually customary to back down, but I didn't. So, I found myself walking to a secluded place behind the bike shed to face him and his peculiar way of punching – I think he was surprised I'd turned up. Again, my judo came in rather handy as I ended up getting him in a headlock on the floor. I remember feeling terrified that he would break free. Before he got that opportunity, we were caught by the science teacher who gave us both a slap around the head and a massive telling off.

Looking back at that incident now, I don't think this boy really disliked me – he just had his reputation to protect, and I was beginning my phase of not backing down!

And then there was an incident that broke my heart – someone who was also picked on by bullies wanted to fight me. I was acting like an idiot and must have annoyed him. As sad as it sounds, I really thought I would be more popular than him, but all I can remember is everyone who surrounded us during our fight cheering for him – I was totally demoralised. Half the school followed me home chanting obscenities as I walked through my front door. My parents wondered what the hell was going on – that was my lowest ever point as a child, finding out how much so many other children hated me, or at least that's the way I perceived incidents like that back then.

What kind of a kid had I turned into, what had got me to this point? It was pure torture and I was lost. Somehow, I kept going, kept putting on my false mask, kept thinking of what I believed was a happy childhood. In fact, I DO think back on it as a happy childhood – there are so many great memories of growing up, so many great holidays and wonderful times with my two brothers and my sister. I love and respected my parents, although we as children must have given them quite a few headaches.

## The return of my bully

I had somehow managed to slowly edge away from the bully who mentally tortured me during that 6-month period I describe in Chapter 1, even if his threat still stalked me. His negative presence continued to loom over me for quite some time after.

However, our paths would cross again when we were paired together on adjoining desks during a year-long series of English lessons at our next school. We must have been about 13 years old. What a feeling of dread when we first sat down together.

It's strange looking back – I can still clearly see the young him and me. Him leaning in towards my ear, his hand covering his mouth, that final whisper before the lesson starts. It will probably have been some subtle reference to one or two of my "faults" but will always have been designed to unsettle and undermine me, cleverly delivering some sharply aimed insult, affecting for the rest of the day how I perceived myself.

Did it work again? Not to the same degree as when I was only eight, although I would be lying if I said it didn't set me back quite a bit.

This time I wasn't alone though. His large ego fed off others too; small comfort back then but the reprieve it afforded me as he cast his net into the pool of weaker minds eased my personal pain.

Turning 16 couldn't have come soon enough, and despite my vulnerability I found myself being really good at rugby. My body was filling out and as I progressed to the age of 18 my bullies seemed smaller and less threatening as I soared to over 6 foot. I was entering adulthood, the real world.

Rugby is the type of sport where participants can vent all their anger and frustration by legally physically hurting someone else, carefully disguised as just a rough tackle. I never played it like that, but I wish I could say the same thing about a few others!

Our team coach used to recruit one or two of the school bullies, and this methodology was often matched by opposing managers. No way was I going to allow myself to be intimidated by young men with problems, as I felt I was better than that – the fightback to reclaim my confidence was on.

I tackled some of these strategically placed bullies on the field of play and scorched past angry wingers to score points. You could say that I was playing a game to taunt some of the bullies who donned a rugby kit. I was athletic and my height helped me to become a fast runner and I used that to my advantage.

The following accounts have been a very difficult part of this chapter to write. They have laid bare some highly personal stuff, including revelations I would have preferred to leave out, as you'll soon read for yourself.

So, for this next section I first needed to seek advice from a behavioural expert on bullying before including them, and she made the call for me.

Dr Lamia is a clinical psychologist and psychoanalyst who has spent 35 years teaching adults, adolescents and pre-teens about dealing with behaviour and emotion. Her young adult book, *Emotions! Making Sense of Your Feelings*, was the recipient of the 2013 Family Choice Award.

According to Dr Lamia, enduring the trauma of being bullied affects people in different ways but fundamentally it entails shame being transferred from the bully to their victim. This is something that can weigh us down for the rest of our lives if we allow it to.

This is a theory or even a truth I had never entertained before and it challenged me to look deeper.

Dr Lamia told me that men in particular who she speaks to years after their ordeals often wish they could go back in time to react differently to those acts of physical abuse. Many men have regretted not hitting back at their bully and struggle to live in the knowledge that they had allowed themselves to be bullied.

I have spoken to an author in the USA, JP Ribner, who often writes articles about his own experiences of being beaten up during his school years. I found one of his moving statements on the online platform Quora, and simply had to track him down to find out more.

Here's part of that article:

"And all those unbearable assholes from my past give me plenty to work with when I'm developing villains for my novels. Oh, and the anger hasn't interfered with my having a life. But it's still there, bubbling deep within me like the red-hot magma in some long-forgotten volcano.

While grass and trees have grown over where the lava once flowed, one never knows when noxious fumes might burst forth, threatening to rob someone's lungs of precious, life-sustaining air.

And no one can be certain when the lava might burst forth from the cone once more, threatening to scorch everything in its path."

I read more about JP to suggest that he still carries feelings of anger towards his bullies, despite the fact that those dreadful experiences have undoubtedly fuelled his own success. And through chatting with the man himself for an hour on the phone, some understandably disturbing revelations came to the surface.

He regretted, as he described, being weak and succumbing to vicious attacks from a number of bullies during childhood, although he confessed that being much smaller than kids in his age group didn't help. So, as a young adult he decided to take up martial arts in order to look after himself. He became an expert in karate and decided to knock on the doors of all of his bullies, one by one, to offer them a rematch. My conversation with JP was clearly taking a different turn, one I hadn't expected.

I am no expert and certainly would never judge the behaviours of past bully victims, some of which are quite understandable considering what they had put up with and I will leave you to be the judge in this instance.

I told JP that I hadn't been expecting him to come out with an angle that looked a fair bit like revenge. With that, he backtracked slightly and I felt he had sensed my unease. He had thought that telling me that any money raised would go to charity might somehow justify what he was doing. I hasten to say that it would appear that no one took him up on his proposal of a rematch.

Did that give him satisfaction, the fact that he got no takers? I sensed not, as his issues didn't appear to have been resolved. JP shared with me that in his case, and he believes this to be true in most cases too, it's once a bully always a bully. He backed up his statement by telling me that the three instigators of violence against him were "nasty pieces of work" who hadn't changed in the slightest.

I asked JP if he thought any of his three former bullies had regretted what they did to him and he snapped back with a firm, "No! I tried getting an apology but only one of them seemed slightly sorry and was more surprised I had taken it so badly."

I can't condone what JP did, but I completely get why he acted this way, and if you have been bullied repeatedly by several people you will share my sympathy for this man too.

During my research for this book, I have learnt that many of those who have bullied others don't realise how it affects their victims unless they are confronted and told by one of them, and it often leaves a feeling of surprise or even disbelief as opposed to regret.

Of course, hearing another victim's story does make you reflect on your own situation, including whether I had regrets about not punching back. My take on it is this: me regretting not fighting back when it started, for me serves no purpose. I come from a loving family and had no understanding or comprehension of violence, so I had up to that point made the assumption that people liked each other. My naivety was my initial downfall, but how could I regret something I didn't have any knowledge about?

Yes, eventually I wised up and made my stand, but it took a few years for that to come to the surface and once it did, I'm not sure I am proud of what then happened! Which brings me onto my dilemma, one that I still wrestle with to this day...

## My dilemma

Firstly, before explaining a bit about my history, which includes a false dose of "fame" and a touch of shame, the upside of my experiences of being bullied have been that I began to develop an empathy for any person or groups of people I would see being taken advantage of. Whether such adversity manifested itself through physical or mental acts of cruelty, violence or something more subtle, didn't matter, I would often choose to react.

However, this upside I just mentioned might not come across as that once you learn how it made me act. Indeed, this has become my cross to bear, my dilemma, and as Dr Lamia advised after I shared it with her, I have to include these accounts in my book. I feel confident that most readers, particularly those who have felt the pain bullying brings, will understand!

I still have mixed up and messed up feelings about opening up and writing this next section, and it has been difficult to live through it all again.

Nevertheless, while what I am going to share isn't the typical behaviour of a past victim of bullying, nor is it uncommon. However, despite my reservations to talk about these things, as my bully behaviour expert advised, it's important to include them, as they provide another perspective and help to balance out the bigger issue surrounding the effects bullying can have on victims, long term.

**These next three stories: hero, fool or villain? I'll let you be the judge!**

These stories are tough to recount, as they bring back sad and bad memories and I hardly recognise the person I was when these events happened. I regret them to this day, but having said that, maybe some good has come from them. I do know that there was no malice involved.

I had left school at 15 with no qualifications to my name. Quite embarrassingly, my mum decided, in her infinite wisdom, to call the owner of a print company in town to see if they had any vacancies for her (lazy) son. Thanks to my mum I landed a factory position with little prospect of moving forward.

Hang on, it's important to stress right now that because of mum's actions, which I didn't appreciate at the time, the road I embarked on in the print trade led to unprecedented success on a scale I could never have imagined. The great thing about my parents was that they weren't at all surprised at my success when it came. Having unquestioning support from two such great people was never lost on me – everyone needs someone, right? I have learnt to count my blessings when they come along!

Anyway, back to the story I've been trying to delay...

## Becoming Loopy

Fast forward 2 years after Mum landed me the job, I must have been 17 going on 18 and had tried really hard to advance my knowledge in print and had worked virtually 12 hours a day, 7 days a week, to please my employers – and loved most aspects of my job.

All seemed to be slowly progressing until one day I nearly blew my chances of a half-decent career altogether. Had this happened in the current era I would have been sacked, and it was only good fortune or luck (call it what you like) that I remained on my rocky journey to becoming the person I was meant to be.

Things had come to a head with the factory bully – he was over 20 stone and used every ounce of his weight to threaten and intimidate the young trainees and apprentices in our company, and he had wrought total havoc in all the time I'd been there. He took a special dislike to me and would often shout me down, humiliate me with sarcasm or physically push me if I didn't toe the line.

And then the crunch day arrived – he confronted me about something and nothing and used words to put me down in front of half the factory workers. I dared to answer something back under my breath and he grabbed a handful of my T-shirt. I didn't know how to react, I felt threatened as he then pushed me back and then I just panicked by striking him clean in his face with my fist. I think I put into that punch what seemed like years of built up frustration. It was like he copped it for all my bullies, past and present.

The force of the punch lifted him off his feet, over the top of an empty pallet and then he landed with a sickening thud on the ground. The next thing I knew he was on all fours begging me not to hit him again. I will never forget that awful gut-wrenching feeling of pity that came over me. He grovelled and was a long way from the overbearing person I had known only a minute earlier. He picked himself up, gathered himself together and told me I'd pay dearly for that. His usual self was returning and that somehow made me feel a little easier.

However, the sad truth is that he never did return to his former self. He had to visit the doctor after the incident and the doctor found something wrong with his heart, which could have killed him if it hadn't been for his timely visit. That proved to be the only good to come out of this awful situation, as he then had three months off work, with ongoing medication that saved his life.

The boss had been away on holiday during this incident, but when he returned, he told me straight that if he had been there that day I would have been sacked on the spot. He then followed up with a comment that is etched into my memory, "And because I wasn't there, well fu***** done, he had it coming!"

That comment left me feeling relieved that I still had my job and confirmed that even my boss thought the bully had received his comeuppance. I didn't know how to react, and this left me feeling confused and vulnerable.

I became a reluctant hero and it made my skin crawl, people associating me with punching the big bully guy at work. They gave me a nickname, "Loopy," like I was crazy, and had a "screw loose" – I felt I had become a cartoon character in the eyes of my work colleagues, who were treating me like some made-up joke character.

I think I was kept on largely due to my willingness to work long hours when most others declined. I was priceless cheap labour and although I should have walked, there was good reason to keep me on the books.

> 66 **My pain may be the reason** 99
> **for somebody's laugh. But**
> **my laugh must never be the**
> **reason for somebody's pain.**
>
> — Charlie Chaplin

The bully returned to work three months later, and we never spoke again. His way of getting back at me was to lock the fire exit door when I frequently nipped out to the shops to grab lunch, which meant that on my return I'd have to walk the long way down the side of the factory to get back in. That made him smile, and strangely enough I never objected, it was like I deserved it and allowed him his moment of daily payback – it was a small price to pay.

If I was filled with resentment and shame for that incident, I never felt the same about this next story, but a pattern was beginning to form...

I caught a bus from work one day into the city centre with my friend Phil; we were both around 20 years old at the time. We had settled on the top deck and it wasn't long before we noticed trouble brewing as three aggressively behaved young guys, two in their early twenties, turned their attention to us. They started to act abusively, particularly towards Phil, who was only around 5 foot 2 and of slight build. They goaded him and basically asked what he was looking at. The two that were older then unleashed the young gun, who lurched in for a kung fu-style kick to Phil's head. I think they were giving him some fighting experience before they waded in themselves. The blow happened so quickly and took us both by surprise, although of course Phil felt the physical pain. The young runt came back for a second kick and I stood up and punched him full on his nose and he immediately backed off. I remember feeling a bit guilty because the kid was only around 17 years old, but he had just attacked my mate and I wasn't going to let that continue despite feeling incredibly vulnerable and afraid.

Their full attention then turned to me and I asked Phil to run (not sure why these words were coming out of my mouth) and with no need for a second prompting, he was off. Two wry smiles presented themselves to me, as the younger bloody-nosed member of the three stepped out of the equation.

The more threatening of the two asked me if I knew who he was, before unleashing two of his best punches to my head. Apparently, and I learnt this later, he was a notorious offender known to the police for drugs and knife crime who held rank in a City gang. Had I known that I probably wouldn't have answered NO to his question or followed up with two punches of my own. He fell to the floor and got up slowly before confessing that no one had ever hit him before. I think I took that as a kind of compliment, but only on reflection, as at that precise moment I was too scared!

I glanced over to notice the bus conductor frozen to his seat with fear – he had witnessed it all but didn't move an inch. A standoff ensued and I was worried one of them might pull a knife. But then, thankfully (for me at least) we heard the siren of a police car, as apparently Phil had raised the alarm. With that, the three guys ran for it and I stayed put.

The result was that I was arrested, along with the young man with whom I'd exchanged fisticuffs, and we were thrown in a cell for many hours. The bus conductor came good with his witness statement and I was released, while the other guy went to prison for a month.

If the nickname Loopy had embarrassed me before, I had now done nothing to warrant a rethink after that escapade! I felt even more like the made-up cartoon character I had become. It was a confusing and rather sad period of my life.

I'd become a reluctant hero yet again and I can't pretend I didn't enjoy some of the attention at first, but I didn't know whether to play down or live up to the reputation bestowed upon me – I was struggling with who I was.

The sad fact as a result of the bus experience was that I could have been badly beaten up or far worse on that bus, but I got away with it, and today I can appreciate that. It frightens me even now to think about what could have been!

Truthfully, I don't regret what I did, but I wouldn't advise anyone to follow my example. I really do think that on another day I might have paid a bigger price.

The outcome might have been so different in this modern era where knife crime is on the rise (up by 16% in 2018 compared to the previous year.) By comparison, back in the 1980s, knife crime wasn't even on the radar.

The third incident centred around a stag night out with friends, some four years later, a few months after I had married Sue.

It was all about drinking and celebrating, from bar to bar we'd planned our route, but no sooner had we got going than we were hounded by a couple of guys in the street. I can only describe them as huge in physique and incredibly intimidating, to the extent that our party of around 20 began to diminish in size, as individuals peeled away one by one. These guys were mocking each one of us as they approached our line, commenting on the way we were dressed – I think we all knew where this was going.

Around 10 of us remained, as one of the two men, after insulting the rest of us, grabbed the youngest member of our entourage, bundled him to his mate, and began roughing him up.

It was another moment where my brain and mouth didn't work as a team because quite out of nowhere, I told them to leave my friend alone, and then added that they should accompany me down the alley next to us to sort out their problem in private.

Was I totally deluded? My heart was racing, but my challenge had been fired off, and it had stunned both men into complete silence. My young friend was released, but unlike in my previous story, he didn't run. By that time the other 8 or so members of our party had sidled away, so we were the only two left and I can't tell you how proud of him I felt as, frightened as he must have been, he chose to stay with me.

We turned into the alley and the two guys seemed hesitant – I was hoping we might talk this one out like sensible adults. No sooner had that thought popped into my frazzled brain than one of them swung his fist at me, but before it took full flight, I knocked him clean out with my own punch.

His friend looked worried and backed off and I was surprised I'd managed to stamp out the threat so easily.

The poor guy didn't move, he was out cold. I hastily made my exit, pulling my friend with me. I jumped into a taxi and my night was over before it had started. In the taxi I stared at my hand and noticed that one of my knuckles on my right hand was cut up badly. It was only then that I realised how hard I must have hit the guy and pondered on what might have happened.

I knew Sue wouldn't approve of what I'd done, despite me feeling that I was defending my young friend and myself, but it didn't wash. Sue deplores any form of violence, and I thought I did too, but I had played my part in a violent act and felt ashamed.

Understandably, Sue was upset and disappointed that I didn't just walk away. More than that, she was concerned that I so easily could have killed the man, especially if he had fallen awkwardly and smashed his head on the ground. "You saw him get up, right?" Sue asked, and suddenly I was overcome with a hot flush. Sue knew from my reaction that I hadn't even given that a thought. How could I be so stupid, I asked myself, and I was consumed with guilt!

> **66 You will never reach higher 99 ground if you are always pushing others down.**
>
> — Jeffrey Benjamin

The idea of me going to prison was a secondary thought to the safety of the person I had hit, but one that scared the living daylights out of me. A night in silence and barely a wink of sleep followed, and although I was met with a hero's welcome when I got into work the next day, I shushed them all up and told them I hadn't exactly covered myself in glory.

I also couldn't help wondering where some of them had been in our moment of need. Some much needed relief then came my way as my young friend told me he went back to check on the guy, and he had got up with the aid of his friend and disappeared into the night.

I was on the receiving end of two weeks of deserved complete silence from Sue. She just wouldn't speak to me and I couldn't blame her. I felt awful, realising that I was no better than the bullies I had encountered. To this day, Sue and I have never spoke about what unfolded that evening, an event which happened over 30 years ago. That was the last time I struck another person.

What do I think of that incident today? I feel that something would have happened that night anyway – my friend was in danger and my instincts had told me that I needed to protect him, regardless of the threat to my own safety. Either my friend or both of us would have been attacked, BUT honestly, even though I'm not so sure just walking away would've been an option, I should have tried – after all I so easily could have ended up inflicting permanent damage, or even killing someone! Better men than me have served time for similar actions, but with far worse outcomes! Maybe there were a dozen ways in which I could have dealt with the situation, and on another night, I could have come up with something more intelligently thought out. However, life doesn't allow us to go back in time, so let's just say I have to live with some regret with this one, and more than a splash of shame too.

I have chosen these three stories, but there had been several others which took place during my pre-marriage years. I had been attacked a few times for trying to stand up to bullies. Sometimes I had talked my friends and myself out of trouble, and on other occasions I had taken a beating. I had even been picked on for being the biggest in my group, with the obvious reasoning that by taking out the main (perceived) threat first, the rest will crumble.

The most recent escapade in my quest to snuff out violence was around 18 months ago. This was to break up a brawl in a club where my son had organised a comedy night. A few young lads started throwing chairs and bottles, it was mayhem – I ran 20 yards to rugby-tackle one of the young men to the ground and held him until he calmed down. He wasn't the instigator, but I had just seen that he'd been cut in the face with broken glass and was full of anger.

So, I wanted to save him from doing something he would regret. Everything eventually calmed down, but it would have quickly escalated had I not intervened.

Sue didn't give me a hard time because I think she knew someone had to do something. There were no bouncers to jump in, but she did remind me that I could easily have been bottled for taking action. I didn't feel like any hero, particularly as my son relived my actions with me later, as apparently I had slipped over in full flight before I made my tackle. It all looked a bit comical as I struggled to keep hold of the muscle-bound guy in my grasp. I remember waving to some friends as they left the hall, thanking them for coming, even as I lay on my back in such a precarious position. I think the cartoon character was making a brief come-back appearance after so many years!

I have no regrets, my intention was honourable, and it was my boy's night, I just hadn't wanted the brawl to overshadow what was an amazing night up to that point.

I wish someone had intervened when I found myself in positions of danger all those years previously, but it just didn't happen that way.

Through all of this, it's important to stress that it isn't in my nature to harm another soul, and even now I have no resentment toward any of the instigators of violence I have come up against. In fact, the main protagonist in the bus incident was almost killed in a stabbing a few years after our encounter, and then I heard he became a reformed character and got a decent job. Without doubt I would be happy to talk to him again over a drink and I am certain that, just like me, he has been through a lot and probably has his regrets too.

I was born into a kind of bubble, wrapped up in the safety of a good home and protected by caring parents, but not everyone has that safety net. We need to understand that some of us are dealt a bad deck of cards at a very young age and it then becomes a matter of knowing how to deal with them throughout our life – we all have a choice, and it can take many years to work it all out and begin to reform.

As an adult, I saw my nemesis.

I came across my "emotionally destructive" bully at a skittles alley when I was in my mid-30s. We sidled past each other and I made sure we didn't make eye contact. This wasn't because I still feared him, but more because one or both of us would have been lost for words had we found ourselves acknowledging each other's presence, especially as both our wives were at our side (or maybe it was his girlfriend).

If I remembered him so vividly for the damage he'd done to my mind over a period of time, I have no doubt that his memories of carrying out that damage would be equally strong. And I would bet my bottom dollar his partner wouldn't approve if he'd started back on his cruel line of patter so vividly familiar to me.

I am mindful of the fact, as I type these words and think back, the boy version of this man, the bully, was always well dressed, charismatic, attractive and every inch a powerful influence at school. I think that even the teachers were in awe of him, especially as he seemed so far ahead of the rest of us pupils in terms of maturity, intelligence and how the world was working.

There is no doubt in my mind that he used all of these talents and character traits to dominate and intimidate those of who didn't have his precocious talents at the time. All this kept his ego fed and gave him free rein to be the bully, without fear of reprisal or comeback.

Imagine if I had approached him that night to remind him of how he had made my life a living hell at school (as if he needed reminding). I saved him the torment and the embarrassment

I knew for sure it would bring him, and that is the difference between us. I wouldn't put even him through that, I've never been the kind to seek revenge. I've moved on in a more positive manner and I hope he has too.

Do I forgive this person for how he made me feel? I am almost certain he wouldn't want my forgiveness, or even think he had done anything to warrant an apology. And I don't harbour good or bad feelings towards him or hold any kind of a grudge.

I decided a long time ago that I wouldn't allow anyone to drain away my positive energy for their own gratification or allow them to place their shame on my shoulders.

In my case it was the emotional bullying I found more difficult to take than the physical stuff, 100-fold. If someone hit me, it wasn't nice, but those types of bullies usually think with their fists. It is those who venture into more of the emotional torment of another human being who are the more calculating. These types of people reach into your mind and prey on your vulnerability, exposing those things about ourselves we would prefer to keep hidden. It's betrayal and victimisation rolled into one, and there's no worse feeling.

If being sensitive, good natured, happy and different is undesirable to certain people, then so be it, I'm guilty as charged. The bullies exploited those precious gifts I was blessed with, that's how it all started for me. And guess what? I am so thankful I clung onto those traits!

Having told my tale, I'm now going to introduce you to other people's stories. I hope you will learn as much from these as I have done.

## Chapter 3

# It is Never the Victim's Fault: Ray Dawson's story

This story might just be the most poignant one in this whole book. The basic essence of Ray Dawson's life isn't about how whether he accumulated monetary wealth as a statement, or reaction to his own sufferings through being bullied, or any form of adversity he has experienced. Ray's wealth and richness is much purer and more meaningful than that. If so far you have assumed that this book might measure success just in one way, read Ray's story, which puts everything into perspective.

Here's how Ray describes himself in one sentence on his LinkedIn profile: "Dedicated to being in the corner of those who feel that no one cares about them in society. And doing so for free."

Ray is a serial volunteer and motivator of others who encourages them to discover and achieve their dreams. He helps people gain self-belief, confidence and motivation, and does it for free because, as he puts it, "Those who need it the most simply can't afford traditional coaching or courses often costing hundreds or even thousands of pounds." Ray is adamant that no one should be excluded from success and happiness because of lack of money!

> 66 **The common mistake that** 99
> **bullies make is assuming**
> **that because someone is nice**
> **that he or she is weak. Those**
> **traits have nothing to do with**
> **each other. In fact, it takes**
> **considerable strength and**
> **character to be a good person.**
>
> — Mary Elizabeth Williams

I wondered what Ray did in his career before he retired that may have qualified him for the invaluable work he does now, and I was impressed with what he shared.

"I left school aged 15 with no qualifications whatsoever. No 'O' levels, **not even a spirit level.**

My working life has encompassed retail, factory, sales, management, training roles. I have done whatever was necessary in life, from being a milkman in the Midlands to acting as company trouble shooter, able to solve problems wherever they arose.

When I decided that I wanted a career in management but had no qualifications or significant experience, I did the logical thing and applied to a company that said both were absolutely essential and got hired without either of them. I think I have always been a bit of a 'go against the grain' kind of bloke. If someone says it can't be done, I see that statement as a challenge.

Following two redundancies, I decided to answer a nagging question in life. Could I have gone to university and gained a degree? So, at 42, I became a full-time mature student. Three years later I attained my BA in Business Administration. It was just a personal challenge. I didn't want to reach old age with that question still hanging there. Did I need the BA? No. Did it help me get jobs? Not really. It just left a three-year gap on my CV!

Forced into early retirement due to serious illness, I considered all the things I had done in life, all the knowledge and skills gained and decided to use them to help others. I knew a lot about motivation; after all, I had recently been to the edge of death as a result of my serious illness and made it back. Getting back to being able to walk a mile took a year. One step, then another, fall down, get up and do an extra step. Simple but excruciatingly painful. Cry me a river didn't even come close. I knew about getting jobs and interviews, so I helped people do that. I knew what it was like to lose your confidence and more importantly, how to get it back and keep it.

So, I helped people do that. I knew I would need contacts to make dreams come true, so I took three years and built a network of people to help with that. In the process, I have become somewhat of a serial volunteer. I encourage others to do that too.

So, what drove me to do the things I have done in life? Partly it was the challenge, not to prove people wrong, but to prove that things can be done with a positive attitude. Did the hurtful words and nastiness I encountered in life from bullies help me to become a stronger person? I'm a bit cautious about this one because not everyone gains strength like that. For some, there are simply no positives that they can find no matter how hard they try. I hope this book will change that.

I would put it like this: In my work, helping people get ready for returning to work, I have often encountered people who have been unemployed as a result of workplace bullying. My experience of how this works and the soul-destroying effects of it have helped me to help them understand that situation and put it behind them."

Ray, now in retirement, has dedicated most of his time in helping individuals to achieve significant changes to their lives on a free-of-charge basis. Free doesn't mean worthless; many people have been helped and they describe the help they have received as priceless. Ray's focus is on mindset change, with highly inspirational and rapid results.

He presents classes in 'Getting back to work' and 'Confidence and Motivation' at a local college and in the community, using his own unique techniques that work. One-to-one support is always available.

While most people in retirement seek a less demanding and more comfortable existence, Ray looks for opportunities to use every ounce of his positivity, born out of past heartbreaks, to improve lives. He is a major driving force for an organisation called Route

66, that was set up to support female victims of domestic violence and abuse.

Ray was invited to become involved in setting up the programme around two years ago. Initially it was to be run by a charity but after their first go at it, Ray was asked to take it on and build it into something bigger and better.

The reason why it hadn't fully worked as a charity was because those who started it *assumed* that every survivor of domestic abuse just needed to get a job in an office, and all would be fine! **Yes, that's what they thought.** Their efforts left one survivor feeling humiliated and in tears and the others there totally switched off, until Ray and a friend (a guest presenter) stepped in and put it right on the day.

So, Ray set about building a series of one-hour guest presenter sessions, where inspirational women from a variety of backgrounds would come in and tell their stories and answer questions. Several have since also become mentors, a vital part of the programme after their graduation ceremony on week six. Twelve hours to totally transform lives and aspirations. Ray describes this as being a wonderful privilege to be able to see such great things happening in a relatively short space of time.

Women who enter the programme have gone on to start businesses, retrain for new careers, return to education and many other things. The presenters keep coming back because, while they sought to bring inspiration, they tend to leave having been completely blown away by the amazing women they have met. Most of all, the women who take part now live their lives entirely on their own terms.

Ray added the following statement: "Our next step is to raise ring-fenced funding for Route 66, with the idea of offering small grants to help our ladies turn their dreams into reality. For those wishing to start a business, we wish to offer funding on the basis that after they have become established, the amount given as seed capital can be donated back to help other ladies in the future. Micro business funding with a heart!"

Although Ray is the only male involved in this programme, all the women have taken this amazing gentleman into their hearts and placed trust in him. He has been able to restore their faith in men and the belief that there are still good guys out there. Considering that some of the women have been close to death at the hands of male perpetrators, Ray finds the trust he is afforded very humbling indeed.

In October 2018, I posted a personal video message on LinkedIn during Anti-Bullying Week. I wanted to put forward something about my own experience and to try and encourage those affected by bullying by explaining how we can turn such adversity into a positive force, and that there is hope.

The response I received was quite astonishing, with my post receiving several thousand views and a high number of comments, likes and shares. People were thanking me for opening up and talking about what many of us feel is a taboo subject. I was direct-messaged with many stories of the hideous experiences victims of intimidation have been through. I felt humbled and challenged, and it was as a result of this strong reaction that I conceived the idea to write this book.

One such person who came forward was Ray, whose story stood out.

Straightaway I felt a strong connection with Ray – his modesty and passion to help people in his community and beyond impressed me. And after sharing with me his own personal story of deep sadness and gross intimidation I wouldn't have blamed him if he'd had just curled up in a ball and resigned from the human race for the rest of his life, but Ray wasn't that type of guy.

Having met Ray and communicated with him on several occasions, I began to think of him as more of a miracle worker – positive, humble and modest beyond comprehension. What stood out for me through getting to know him, and quite literally I had to force him to open up about this, is that he has given all his time and help at great financial cost to himself. He has often dipped into his pension to support those who he felt needed a motivational gift to spark the change in mindset he felt they needed. A few days before last Christmas, Ray called me like an excited child, almost losing his breath as he speedily fired off his words, to report that he'd just bought a computer as a Christmas present for a young boy whose mum couldn't afford to buy it herself.

Knowing that Ray didn't have an endless stream of funds himself I asked how he would get through Christmas having less himself. He just told me that there could be no greater gift for him than having the privilege of being able to change someone else's Christmas and affect their life positively. I could tell from the way Ray told me this that this wasn't an exaggeration. The boy desperately wanted to learn and study, so he was moved to tears when his computer arrived, and his mum was ecstatic beyond what many of us might comprehend. Ray, whose wife had sadly passed away a few years ago, spent his Christmas alone, but he probably felt more fulfilled than many of us who enjoyed plentiful company, comforts and possessions over and above what we truly need.

Whenever I speak to Ray and try to squeeze out these amazing nuggets of true wisdom, and probe for the great things he has done for others, he is hit by a dilemma which I totally understand. To him, it's like he is blowing his own trumpet and he doesn't want to be thought of in that way. He feels uncomfortable because he just does his best. "You are truly a special person," I told him once, and although I felt he was flattered, he was also a tiny bit embarrassed and tried to bat those words back to me. "Ray," I said, "You have helped me to heal a part of my heart by sharing your stories and you must do it again to help more people." He said that he wanted to and although he was apprehensive about opening up his own wounds, it wasn't long before he sent me his first draft, peppered with his usual modesty. I told him that he needed to go deeper and if possible lay bare the difficulties he had experienced in the past.

I asked him to live through the emotions and sadness he had felt, so that we could know, or at least start to know, how he had got to where he is now. So, I feel very privileged that he has agreed to do this.

# Here's Ray's story...

My first experience of being bullied was when I was probably about six or seven years old. I loved to play in the old motor coach in the scrapyard and though it wasn't allowed, I did it anyway. I was a child after all!

On my way home one day, I was surrounded by a small but menacing gang and frogmarched off to see the 'leader'. Their grip was so tight around my arms, it really hurt. I had bruises later but told my mum I had fallen over. It appeared that I had inadvertently entered their territory. This was back in the mid-1950s, so if anyone out there thinks gang culture is a new phenomenon, think again. In order to be allowed to leave, a forfeit would have to be paid, a dare to be done or some stupid thing. Then mention was made of some unspeakable acts others had done to gain membership. Even at that tender age, I was terrified by this and made a break for it. Looking back, I had a very lucky escape because those acts were of a sexual nature.

I now realise that the leader and certainly those gang members in his 'inner circle' were paedophiles. I never went back to that part of town. I also never forgot their faces or their names. I can tell you that not one of them ever amounted to much in life. They are gone now but the impact their bullying ways had on me is clear because as I write this, I could be right back there as if it was today. It really hurts to write this but it's the only way that bullying will be stopped. It wasn't my fault. **It is never the victim's fault.**

Around three years later, I began to get picked on by a boy called John. We were in the same class at school and while I was a bookworm, he was always messing around. I was also a bit, shall we say, rotund. Two perfectly good reasons in his eyes to go after me. I would get tripped up. Water would be poured on my homework, which was serious stuff in the days before permanent ink!

We were a poor family and sometimes my shoes would be too small, meaning my toes would hurt. He knew this and would wait for the chance when no one was looking and stamp on my feet, just to see the tears forming. My clothes were sometimes too tight or worn out with holes in and boy, did he make fun of me for that. He would come up behind me and pull my hair just to let me know he could and that there was no hiding place from him. I lived in fear every day.

One day, he tripped me up on the school stairs and, looking back, I could easily have died if I hadn't been able to stop myself from falling three steps down with fifteen more solid stone steps to go. I genuinely thought he was going to finish the job with a swift kick, but a teacher came around the corner and yes, you guessed it, said, "Get up Dawson, stop fooling around!" John mimicked the teacher's voice and repeated those words.

Then there were the personal, hurtful words, oh yes, lots of them came my way. He would call me fatty and mock me with what he probably thought were funny imitations of me struggling for breath when trying to climb the rope ladder in PE. I had serious bronchial problems as a child and spent more than one Christmas confined to bed. I suffer with them even now.

One day I plucked up the courage to ask him why he picked on me. That is when the basic truth about bullies came out and it has stuck in my mind ever since. "Why do you pick on me and bully me like you do?" I asked. "Because I can," was the reply. And that was his truthful answer. This went on for some time, then one day, I just couldn't take it anymore. I had tried throwing a sickie a few dozen times but that didn't work with my Mum anymore. I couldn't tell her; it just wasn't an option back then.

Not far from home, there was a railway line where steam trains would hammer by, belching steam. All the children would watch them rush past. I watched them too, but one day an awful thought came into my mind. In truth, it had been there for a while, slowly growing and gathering strength. You see, a few months earlier, an old lady had reached a desperate point in her life and had chosen to end it all by lying on the tracks. There was nothing the engine driver could do. She died. The bullying had become so intense that I too wondered if this was a way to escape. That is how bad it got for me.

If you have never experienced the corrosive effects of bullying on confidence and self-esteem, you may well find it hard to understand how such a young mind could reach this point. To be thinking that the only escape might be death. That leaving this world and those you love for a place unknown, how this could ever be an attractive option. The answer is, EASY.

Every word, every trip, every trick and every insult accumulated because it was relentless but often subtle. That's how bullies do it, out of sight so no one knows. They start with the physical, hit you with the emotional and then they are in your head and eventually, they can overwhelm you. So others didn't see it. In my own mind, there was no one to turn to, no one in my corner as it were.

I had older brothers and a sister but back then, if I had spoken to them, they might have waded in and when they had gone, the bully and I would still be there, victim and nemesis, preparing for round 100. Why on earth would I let myself think things like this because of a bully? Looking back, it seems silly, but back then it was all too real. I was literally six feet from going for it. I nearly did but thankfully, the train roared by, shaking the ground I was stood on. Sadly, telling others what is happening is still not always an option, which may account for why so many youngsters take their own lives.

Next day, he went for me again and out of the blue, I just shouted at him at the top of my voice and everyone around suddenly knew what John had been doing to me, including some very sheepish looking teachers. They already knew but had chosen to do nothing. They could have. **They should have**. I guess I had nothing to lose because I was at the end of my tether, I really was.

Then the strangest thing happened. He left me alone for a period of some weeks. Peace reigned, but in the back of my mind, I feared that it wouldn't last. Bullies do that sometimes too. They allow a false sense of security to build then wham, back they come. A kind of good cop, bad cop all in one. One day he spoke to me and I told him again just how bad he had made me feel, how my life had become unbearable. And he said sorry. We talked for a while and when we moved schools, he even became a sort of 'friend'. I remember him telling me that he was regularly beaten by his father at home and that this made him feel angry. So I became the focus for all his anger. He didn't tell me that as an excuse, just an insight into how awful his life was. Rightly or wrongly, it didn't cut much ice with me. There are simply no excuses. Those excuses don't help the victims now lying in cemeteries, do they?

Nothing else of note happened for years until the sad loss of my son to still-birth late in the pregnancy. Everyone at work was very understanding. Then out of the blue, one of the managers decided to make me his target. I would be ridiculed, singled out for attention and his words cut me like a knife, it was heart-breaking. I was dealing with a painful loss and right at that point this man used my weakened state to bully me in any way he could. Truly unforgivable behaviour. He even gave me a nickname. A stupid name but even now, I can't bring myself to share it. I began to dread going into the office. I loved the job and the industry. I loved helping my clients. The rest of the staff seemed great. But they were also blind and deaf. How else can I explain why they said and did nothing when the ridicule cascaded down upon me in group meetings?

The homeless often say they gain a superpower when they are on the streets. They become invisible and that's why people walk by as if they weren't there. I totally understand that feeling because I had it too. When I had recovered from the grief, the day came when I felt able to challenge his behaviour. I told him how his words and his open ridicule of me really hurt and that I was not prepared to let it go on. He had no explanation to offer. He did it because he could and that was good enough for him. That old chestnut reared its ugly head once more. I think this happens much more often than people admit, especially in the workplace.

But to speak out is seen as a sign of weakness, which of course is so wrong. Most days now, if you pick up a newspaper or watch the news on TV, you will see and hear about yet another person who has been bullied to death. The people who knew them always say the same things. "We didn't know, we thought he or she was worried about exams, if only they had spoken up, we could have helped". In other words, it wasn't their business, and that's what needs to change and fast. **This needs to become everyone's business.** We have to ask questions. Voice our concerns. Speak out or forever live with the regret that comes from doing nothing. Young or old, lives are important and we have already lost too many who may have gone on to achieve wonders in life. We will never know.

My workplace bully did become remorseful and apologised but you can't ever take back words that have left scars on the other person's heart and soul. I was a physically strong man, confident enough to take on many challenges in life, but he saw his chance when I was at my weakest point and my tank of resistance was empty.

Now at 68, I am out of it, retired. But the scars of my experiences mean that if I find examples of bullying, I always challenge it. If someone is feeling near to the edge because of bullying, I simply will not back away from helping them. **Bullying has to be stopped.**

When my daughter was bullied badly at school, emotionally and physically, the teachers came down on the side of the bully, saying they had a difficult life. That happens a lot in their quest not to rock the PC boat – they live on. So, I took her out of school and taught her myself instead. Teachers, it appears, also live in fear of bullying parents. How stupid is that? Spine and grow one comes to mind.

It was only after taking her out of school that more facts came out. It seems that one teacher in particular delighted in locking her in a cupboard or keeping her in at lunch times, so she didn't mix with the other children.

At a previous school, she had been shunned by the other children because, "Your mum has cancer and it's catching". Sadly, this ridiculous and hurtful lie took hold in some of the more ignorant parents' minds too, so she never got invited to parties. I only discovered later that those original words had been spoken by a teacher! A lie and a misconception, that's enough to get bullied for. And she was.

How sad that in the 21$^{st}$ century, the spectre of bullying still looms large. We talk about anything and everything these days, yet we fight shy of this one until it is too late and another casualty results.

In recent years, I have been very fortunate to be able to help female survivors of domestic abuse to build a new life on their own terms. Many have suffered terrible treatment, physically, mentally and emotionally. It is one of the worst forms of bullying and I abhor it. It is a cowardly act.

When I was a very small boy, I witnessed domestic violence first-hand, and all these years later it still happens in society. Why is that? Back then, it was accepted as normal behaviour, a 'domestic', the police used to call it. **Nothing to see here; move along, it's not**

**your business**. I remember my Mum screaming at me and saying, "Go and fetch the neighbour, your Dad's going to kill me!". Imagine how awful that was for a small boy. But it got worse because when I hammered on the neighbour's door, they answered and I cried out for help, repeating my Mum's words. The neighbour said, "She probably deserves it" and slammed the door on a little boy with tears streaming down his face. I had to dash back into the house not knowing what I would find. Mum dead? Mum lying there severely injured? Wearing another black eye? That's the truth about domestic violence.

Those who do it are bullies and cowards. They are nothing less. When I was a little older and one inch taller, I stood in the middle and stopped it. His fist went back as if to hit me, but it never landed. And that was the last time a finger was laid on Mum. It took a boy to do what men like the neighbour could have done. But it wasn't his business.

And that is why today over 2 million women in the UK and hundreds of thousands of men suffer in silence from domestic abuse. Because it isn't 'our' business. But things are changing. There is a welcome drive now to make it everyone's business, so that victims can speak out and become survivors. The police see it as their business now.

I believe that is how bullying needs to be perceived. **It is everyone's business.** People are speaking out, telling their stories and the public are waking up to the bad things that have always happened and are finally beginning to say enough is enough. Children are now being bullied online, even to the extent of terrible self-harm or taking their own lives. Now the bullies want to watch as their handiwork leads to yet another loss to society and a family who will spend their lives asking why they didn't know what was happening. We all have a part to play in stopping this. That is why this book is a milestone, a marker in the sand that says, **"This has to stop"!**

If my story has made one person believe that they don't have to put up with it, or, and here is an optimistic thought, if a bully has read this and thought that maybe it isn't such a smart to do after all, well, job done. But it will only end when we have honest and open conversations about it. This book has started those conversations. **Let's make ending bullying all of our business.**

---

*That's the end of Ray's story – thank you for opening up your old wounds and sharing those memories.*

Reading all the stories in this book, I feel that Ray has struggled more than anyone else to put himself in the shoes of his bullies and offer any kind of understanding as to why they subjected him to such dreadful acts of physical and mental harm. Yet, having said this, I think he is at the top of the pile in terms of dedicating his life to making sure that as many socially excluded and "disadvantaged" people as possible who he seeks to draw alongside, won't go through what he went through... and to me that is the epitome of success.

It's disturbing for me to read about how close Ray was to that train track when thoughts of ending it all were hijacking his mind. Yet at the same time I know he has used that experience to help quite a few people on the brink of suicide come back from their hell. Yes, this kind gentleman has not only helped save lives but also enriched them too!

Ray has also impacted positively on so many individuals by helping their wishes come true, just by listening to what their dreams are and going all out to make sure they happen. He helps people believe in themselves and has dipped into his own pocket several times to pay for this to happen. The most recent email I received spoke of his joy in taking a survivor of domestic violence to sing at a studio.

"She was so good", he told me, "that they asked for her voice to be recorded and included on an artist's audio."

The lady thanked Ray and told him she has never experienced kindness like this from anyone else in her whole life.

He also writes CVs for those who struggle to find jobs, and he has helped many transition into jobs they thought they couldn't get.

Ray's experience of being bullied at work after the stillbirth he and his wife suffered several years ago, is hard to understand; that this bully took advantage of his weakness during such a tough period in his life. How brilliant then that Ray somehow got through all that to be the positive influence he is now.

My bully expert Dr Mary Lamia sent me some articles she wrote, and part of one spoke to me about Ray's situation at work, and it might resonate with you too:

"Bullies are notorious for misusing power. They may overtly denigrate, criticize, or exclude you in such a way that, at the time, you may be incapable of responding. In a group meeting, they may covertly destroy you by responding to a comment or suggestion you make, with a remark alluding to the idea that they don't understand what you are talking about—suggesting that you are inarticulate or ignorant—and not allow for clarification. But even more insidious is their capacity to manipulate or incite others to be aggressive, belittling, or hostile toward you through their denigrating remarks or creation of rumours. The farther they push you down, the more they rise to the top. And they do succeed.

Shame is what bullies attempt to hide; they have high self-esteem but are very shame-prone— they are about the exposure of their failures or shortcomings. Their mean behaviour towards others keeps their self-esteem high because it takes their own and others' attention away from the parts of themselves about which they are ashamed of. Thus, the bully gives away his shame by denigrating you and, as a result, a bully will make you experience shame about your own inadequacies. This will relieve him of any anxiety that his own shame will be exposed. And you will be left experiencing anxiety and humiliation."

It was interesting that Ray challenged his work bully about his behaviour and the bullying stopped. I also agree that his colleagues staying quiet and not taking his side was disappointing, but I also know first-hand the power a bully has over more than one person in a room. How many times have we seen TV footage or read in the news about bystanders being frozen to the spot as someone is verbally or physically attacked?

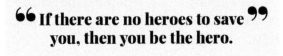

**66 If there are no heroes to save 99 you, then you be the hero.**

— Denpa Kyoshi

So, having suffered immeasurable sadness and reached unimaginable lows, how has Ray turned those negative influences into the positive energy that feed so many others who have experienced significant trauma and misfortune?

Here's what I think, having known and communicated with him for over a year.

Without doubt, Ray has a kind heart and is mild mannered, and that has been his problem (no, someone else's problem) and also the making of the man!

The good conquered evil, if you like!

Ray, like most of the others highlighted in this book, has been taken advantage of for his gentle and quiet nature. He was an easy target because of the attributes he possesses of which we should all celebrate, but as we know bullies sadly exploit such virtues and use them to their advantage.

Ray now demonstrates self-deprecation but is actually charming and humble with it. This is as a result of the huge knocks he's picked up; lacking in self-confidence because of how he's been treated. Like me, he still finds it a bit hard to deal with praise or compliments. That's not what I deem to be a negative trait in this instance, far from it.

Here's the crux of the matter:

At some point Ray chose not to be embittered and sour as a result of all his negative experiences. Instead he flipped these on their head to use every ounce for good. I think this not only feeds those lost souls he helps mend but his own soul to, I am convinced of that!

Here is some additional information you may find useful, taken from the Bullying UK website, bullying.co.uk

# The signs of workplace bullying

If you feel as though you are experiencing bullying in the workplace, this can be a very devastating and distressing issue. You may be feeling very low and anxious at the thought of going to work and facing the individual or group that may be subjecting you to this. Workplace bullying can take shape or form in many different ways. You may be questioning whether what you are going through is workplace bullying and a lot of this depends on if you actually are feeling bullied or harassed by a particular individual or a group of people. There are many instances of bullying behaviour in the workplace, such as the following:

- Being constantly criticised, having duties and responsibility taken away without good reason
- Shouting, aggressive behaviour or threats
- Being put down or made to feel like the butt of the jokes
- Being persistently picked on in front of others or in private
- Being constantly ignored, victimised and excluded regularly
- Constantly mocking and attacking members of staff
- Spreading malicious rumours about members of staff
- Misuse of power or position to make someone feel uncomfortable or victimised
- Making threats about job security without any basis or substance
- Blocking promotion or progress within the workplace

These are just a few signs of bullying and there are many more and it is dependent on the organisation or the industry too. Unfortunately, bullying can take its toll on your health and wellbeing. If you do feel that you are under duress, please do make an appointment with your GP so that you are able to get support for this. It is important to keep a diary of all incidents with times, dates, witnesses and what happened. This will help you enormously, especially if you decide to take this further.

If you are feeling bullied, confide in a manager or the Human Resources department in your workplace. This might not be so easy to do if it is a small organisation or you are being harassed or bullied by a manager. You could ask if they have a policy in place to deal with bullying and harassment at work. If you are a member of a trade union, you could get in touch with them and ask them for advice and representation. If you have house insurance, then you may be covered for legal expenses too, it's worth checking this.

# Chapter 4

# Unleash Your Awesome!: Taz Thornton's Story

Taz Thornton popped up on YouTube while I was typing something about motivational speaking. It had occurred to me that at the ripe old age of 55, having written my first book, and about to embark on my second, that maybe I should start to learn how to articulate some of the important and serious messages I want people to hear about and learn from... that is if ever someone should be so kind as to ask!

Taz was holding an audience like I'd never quite witnessed, and I was more than a little curious. Usually when I see and hear a speaker I scan for the flaws, the stutters, the loss of confidence and the awkwardness that others might not detect. I think I must do this because public speaking is something I would love to do but also one of those things I fear almost as much as death itself! Maybe, subconsciously, I was looking for reasons and excuses not to go out and grab a speaking gig.

But there were no flaws with Taz; just an articulate, intelligent and well-constructed talk about how those of us listening might Unleash our Awesome, despite most of us thinking we haven't got it in us.

Her meaningful and inspirational message struck a chord and spoke to me, as profoundly as anyone who has battled back from problems of the past. Yes, I knew there must have been some BIG roadblocks she'd encountered and overcome; she had more than hinted about such issues. I watched more of her videos – this lady was mending people's hearts after opening up their minds, and she cared, I mean really, really cared!

The lady with the pink hair and pink framed glasses captivated her audience and demonstrated empathy and compassion for every "hurting" soul in the room. I think that in situations where people shut off from the normal rigours of daily routine to listen to a speaker of such authority and authenticity as Taz they find their hurt even if they didn't quite know it was in them.

And after coming across one of her TEDx talks, more was revealed where she admitted, rather disturbingly, that at one point when she had hit that low, how she had prayed to whatever gods might be listening for that terminal illness to come. And when it didn't come how she would take risks, and if she was still alive then someone must still want her to be here. So, here's what else can be found out about this remarkably positive Lady from Lincolnshire, who's life hasn't always been a bed of roses.

Taz Thornton has been there, done it and seen it in ways that will make you change your view of the world and want to do better. As a high-flying corporate director, she appeared to have the world in her palm – nobody could see her crumbling beneath the pinstripes. She rebuilt after breaking her back at 21, then fought back after the breakdown at 33 that saw her seeking wisdom from shamans and medicine people, as well as using everything in her NLP and coaching toolkit to reconstruct her life. That breakDOWN turned out to be Taz's breakTHROUGH, and she's now impacting people far and wide as the UK's #1 Inspirational Breakthrough Speaker, best-selling author, seminar leader and coach.

A few weeks later we hooked up through LinkedIn and I checked out her posts and was blown away by the numbers of her followers. There were likes, comments and shares like they were going out of fashion. I wasn't at all surprised as to why so many people had latched onto her words of wisdom, it's just rarely seen in this type of forum! The lady can put together single sentences of such profoundness that the reactions are instant, and always consistently well received by the many who let their reactions be known.

Taz had also made her social media video content current, relevant and incredibly interesting too, and I detected this charismatic powerhouse, with her "Unleash Your Awesome" slogan clearly visible on her T-shirt, had a deep-rooted, painful angle to her story which had inspired her to put herself out there.

I always wonder what backstory those who excel at something so passionately actually is – there's always something!

A few weeks later, Taz commented on a LinkedIn video post I put out that told a little of my story about me being bullied as a child. Her words were encouraging and welcome, particularly for someone who struggles with pointing their face into a cameraphone, and I was flattered. She direct messaged me with some comments about my video touching her and how her own personal suffering at the hands of bullies throughout her life had taken its toll.

Without hesitation I messaged Taz to tell her about my book and without needing to hear all her details I just asked if she could contribute something of her personal story, including how she got to be the successful, influential person she is now.

We did the Skype meet up and I remember being mesmerised by her charm, and how relaxed and open she was. A lady after my own heart I thought as she held a mug of coffee and proceeded to sip away. That was my cue to pull over my own mug of coffee, hidden out of screen shot and follow suit. Can't say I've done a 2-way coffee indulging Skype session before, but I highly recommend it. Seems we both share the same addiction!

> 66 **People who repeatedly attack** 99
> **your confidence and self-**
> **esteem are quite aware of your**
> **potential, even if you are not.**
>
> — Wayne Gerard Trotman

I listened to her accounts of being emotionally bullied throughout different stages of her life, through school, through an abusive relationship, and without her even telling me I just knew the weight of all that baggage had long since left her. Takes one to know one, right?

I noted her lack of emotion when sharing some tough stuff. I recognise that in me too, maybe it's an outward sign that we are both seriously done with being upset by our bullies of the past, and that they hold no more power over us.

Taz hadn't documented too much about her experiences of being bullied at school and it is this she wanted to focus on in this chapter. She was all but onboard, pending knowing more about my book's purpose.

Taz wrote her own book, *Unleash Your Awesome*, and I immediately ordered my copy, and it confirmed how she'd used all the adversity in her life to fuel her passion to make sure stuff like that wouldn't hold other people back – I was impressed! We chatted openly and warmly, acknowledging each other's pain before our situations turned.

I think there is an instant respect between people who have suffered bullying and who have got through it when they begin to engage in conversation. It's as though we know what the other person is thinking. Our meeting was even more confirmation that we need to help people who've suffered oppression, to help them rethink how they can use what happened as a force for a new positive beginning.

Taz, now married to her wife Asha, and with the break-up of previous, destructive relationships behind her, is happier than ever, and she knows exactly who she is and what her purpose on this Earth is all about.

Taz wrote about her moving story and incredible journey in her book, and I was so inspired by her undeniable gift for painting the pictures of her life with words, and I told her so.

Unlike me, Taz is extremely articulate, and can speak her story as well as she writes about it, and one day I hope she can help nudge me into my discomfort zone to address such things, over a few coffees of course!

# Here's Taz's story...

**How 'bullying' taught me to flip my negatives and Unleash My Awesome!**

I can still remember feeling terrified as all the big girls, from the year above mine, crowded into the mobile classroom.

I'd tried, again, to break away from the 'friend' who'd been bullying me since primary school, and she'd called in the big guns to scupper my plans.

It was in the 80s. I was about 12 years old and the only one in the classroom when they all filed in, pulled up plastic school chairs and sat in a circle around me – effectively blocking my escape route.

If I allow myself to go there, I can hear the sounds of chairs being pulled across the floor, and that dull thud as they sat themselves down, forming a wall of aggression.

They sat in silence for a moment, staring me down. I felt tiny. There was nowhere to go. Nobody was coming to my aid. I wouldn't be able to talk my way out of this one, and I certainly wouldn't be able to fight my way past half a dozen or so second year girls.

On the face of it, the 'pal' I was trying to break away from had been my best friend since primary school. Or, at least, that's the way it looked on the surface.

We'd speak for hours on the telephone every night – I'd sit on my parents' stairs and call just after Neighbours. We sat next to each other on the bus and together in class. We spent time together outside of school. Looking back, I can see the relationship was toxic, and if I'd only had the courage to stand up for myself, perhaps I could have escaped all those stand-offs with the bigger kids and painful, brain-shaking slaps around the head from my so-called 'bestie' if I put a foot out of line.

As it happened, a foot out of line was trying to make friends with someone other than her. Or not calling. Or not wanting to spend every available moment with her.

Most of the time, I complied – it was easier to just put up with things than to make a fuss and end up being hit or bullied – but, every so often, I'd find a dose of courage and try to create change.

That's how I came to be on my own, in a mobile classroom, surrounded by the year two mafia.

My 'bestie' was nowhere to be seen, but at the very heart of the proceedings.

The ringleader made it very clear who they were there to 'protect' and demanded to know why I was trying to stop being friends with her. They told me, in no uncertain terms, that I was to remain her best friend and stop trying to break away. The consequences would be dire if I tried to leave the friendship again.

I don't remember how long I was there for, but I still remember their faces and, if I concentrate really hard, I can bring some names to mind as well.

I tried so many things to break free.

My mother heard my crying one day, and I ended up confessing all. Together, we hatched an elaborate plot. I was to call my friend and ask her to please stop hitting me around the head, and my mum would 'overhear' and then take the phone from me and speak her mind. The plan worked perfectly, but it only made things worse.

I remember another time, in English class, where something inside me finally snapped and I stood up. I felt, for sure, that I was about to punch my bullying 'bestie' square on the nose, but my moment of glorious courage was short-lived. The other kids must have picked up on the energy and, by the time they'd crowded around chanting "Scrap! Scrap! Scrap!", the teacher had marched across and broken up the melee before any fists had been flung.

Things calmed for a while after my dear mum came up with another plan. Her best friend's niece was in year three – a year above my bully's teenage wall of protection – and she was happy to have a quiet word in their shell-likes and warn them off.

Eventually, I shook off my bully when the time came to move on to the next school. With my parents' help, we managed to secure me a place at the grammar in the next town – just beyond the normal catchment area and away from the confining 'friendship' that had kept me down since my schooldays began.

Looking back on my life now, I don't regret a single thing, though it's fair to say that the 'bullying' theme has raised its ugly head on several occasions.

Today, in my work as a coach, speaker and trainer, I'm passionate about helping others to stand their ground and step into their power – I'm pretty sure my own experiences have helped me to inspire and support others. Certainly, I can empathise on a different level to those who've never experienced oppression first-hand.

If I was to sketch out a timeline, there would be several points on my life map that could come under the heading of 'bullying'.

I was 'bullied' a little at grammar school but learned to give off an air of assertiveness that meant most people left me alone – I never actually raised my fist, though people probably thought I would at the drop of a hat.

I felt bulled by a couple of teachers – including one who told my classmates I'd amount to nothing and used me as an example of what not to aspire to.

I went through a horribly abusive relationship, which led to me going into hiding to escape and took years to recover from emotionally.

If I look back at some of my positions during my career, I could certainly add bullying bosses to the list as well.

And, in later life, I ended up in a very controlling 'friendship' that pretty much emulated the one from my early school days.

It took lots and lots of personal development – including a decade spent learning from shamans and medicine people – to rebuild and rediscover my true self and my confidence. I had built up so many layers of armour – so many masks – that **it took an emotional breakDOWN to break THROUGH.**

Sometimes, people struggle to understand how I can be so grateful for that breakdown. Those dark times really were the pits and, certainly, I didn't think I wanted to be alive at the time; indeed, I hatched plans to check out on more than one occasion.

However, if I hadn't hit rock bottom, I wouldn't have had such solid ground to push back up from. If I hadn't broken down enough for all the baggage I'd been carrying to flood out, I might never have been able to rebuild myself into the shape I was always meant to be.

Through those challenging times, I learned how to flip my negatives – how to find a positive, a life lesson, through every difficult situation. It's one of my core beliefs now: life doesn't happen TO us, it happens FOR us and, if we can just learn to look at our rich tapestries from a different angle, all kinds of possibilities and growth opportunities start to appear.

I've also come to believe that, through all the trials and tribulations we face, we each have one, big, overarching theme to learn about in this lifetime. Every now and then, we'll get a little test – a prod from God, the universe, fate, whatever you believe is out there – to check we're still growing, learning and staying on track.

If I try to home in on my big lesson, it would be so easy to label it 'bullying'. Instead, I choose to see it in a different way – same teachings, different angle.

If I identify as being a victim of bullying, I'll hold myself in that energy. If, as an adult, I identify those who challenge me as 'bullies', I give them power over me – the very word immediately puts them in a position of 'oppressor', and nobody's oppressing me now, thank you very much.

Whenever I find myself in that kind of position with another person, I pause and ask myself how and why I've invited them into my life. I ponder on the teaching: why have I manifested this? What is it here to teach me and how can I take the best possible course of action for all involved?

Once I do that, once I get some perspective, I can gain so much.

It stops being about someone controlling me or dictating my actions and becomes an opportunity for self-reflection and growth. Time to stretch that comfort zone, baby!

So, my life theme isn't about being bullied. Instead, I say it's about learning to step into my power and unleash my awesome.

The same could be just as true for you.

**So, that's Taz Thornton's powerful story, which we can all learn a lot from, not least how she successfully managed to get to a position in her life, after often finding herself the victim, where she flatly refused to be the victim of bullying anymore.**

There was something important that interested me about her earlier life as I noted that her situation at school started to eventually improve as a result of sharing her bullying dilemma with her mum. This really does emphasise the fact that sharing with another person in such difficult circumstances can often be critical to a positive outcome.

It was disconcerting to learn that Taz's success as a businesswoman didn't lead to happiness, as she was still hoping and praying that somehow her life would end. However, Taz is living proof that no matter how dire and desperate our situation might be, there is a way, with a little help, to turn everything around. These words she wrote really resonated with me: "If I hadn't hit rock bottom, I wouldn't have had such solid ground to push back up from."

The bullying I endured didn't lead to suicidal thoughts, but I feel it contributed to temporarily damaging my mind in other ways. Looking back, I think I was guilty of self-loathing and one quick fix remedy was to binge drink for a few years in my mid to late teens. I thought this would turn a timid me into a super sociable, interesting and more attractive version, but of course it did nothing of the sort! In fact, this lifestyle almost led to my premature death at 19. I was knocked over by a car outside my local pub after consuming copious amounts of alcohol. The surgeon who stitched me back together was surprised when I made it through.

> **❝ People try to say suicide is the ❞**
> **most cowardly act a man could**
> **ever commit. I don't think that's**
> **true at all. What's cowardly is**
> **treating a man so badly that**
> **he wants to commit suicide.**
>
> — Tommy Tran

Of course, none of that directly happened as a result of me being bullied at school, but it does raise questions about the insecurities I suffered.

Brad Burton, the UK's number one motivational business speaker (who is a dear friend of Taz's) often quotes this sentence, "Every decision you have ever made in your entire life has led you to this moment."

Brad talks about those big NOW WHAT moments in our lives that change everything, those rare occasions that are life defining, where making the right choice at the right time might be critical to our existence. Without doubt, my accident was my NOW WHAT moment. It changed the course of my life for the better, as it became the moment when I had to grow up and take some responsibility for my own actions.

I think that, just like Taz, I had hit rock bottom, and there was only one direction I wanted to travel in. I was fortunate enough, maybe through luck, to be given another chance.

Selfishly, I had put myself and my family through the heart-breaking ordeal of my accident and this was my wake-up call. It made me realise that I wanted much more than my life was offering me back then. Even though it would take me a few more years to get there, at that point a switch had been thrown.

I have spoken to a few people whose experiences of being bullied are still raw, mainly because the ordeals they've suffered have been more recent. Some suffer depression, or at least still massively feel the effects of what happened to them and find it hard to think their situation will ever change for the better.

One young man told me over the phone he'd attempted suicide because he lost his confidence to work, he was verbally bullied and abused at his last job and walked out because there wasn't any support from his employers. He then felt a huge responsibility to apply for jobs, and as the months ticked by, he began to yield to the full force of pressure piling up on top of him, as thoughts of suicide crowded his mind.

Ultimately, in hindsight, he knew he had made a massive mistake in attempting to take his own life and can't comprehend how he nearly deprived his wife of a husband and his children of a father.

Thankfully, he started to talk to his wife and a close friend, and with their support got the right medical help from his doctor. His mental wellbeing is still far from stable but is under control and he puts that largely down to how his wife has helped him through the darkest chapter of his life. If only he could have found it in him to speak to her before he tried to end his own life; he knows he should have.

That's the message I want to focus on right now – if you are suffering because of the victimisation you have endured, or are still enduring, please TALK TO SOMEONE about your situation. Don't try and take it all on yourself and deprive the opportunity of someone close to you, or someone professionally trained, in helping you to figure it out.

When Taz hit her lowest point, she sought help and that included her looking at ways to heal spiritually. She looked into and later studied shamanism and its medicines, which helped to transform her situation. Sometimes almost yielding to death can switch to fighting desperately for life, but it often requires a helping hand.

I have received quite a lot of messages and have spoken to people who are at or near to rock bottom right now, who have made the effort to thank me for helping to open up this whole terrible reality that is happening in front of our noses, day in, day out. And when I listen, I find it terribly difficult to know what to say. There isn't a quick fix answer, but there is always a way, there is always hope. This is why I wrote this book, so I can bring stories like Taz's into the open to show those who are spiralling into depression or experiencing suicidal thoughts to take inspiration from others who have been in those dark and murky places, so they might also find a way forward.

HelpGuide.org is a non-profit mental health and wellness website which offers this helpful advice:

# Don't keep these suicidal feelings to yourself

Many of us have found that the first step to coping with suicidal thoughts and feelings is to share them with someone we trust. It may be a family member, friend, therapist, member of the clergy, teacher, family doctor, coach or an experienced counsellor at the end of a helpline. Find someone you trust and let them know how bad things are. Don't let fear, shame or embarrassment prevent you from seeking help. And if the first person you reach out to doesn't seem to understand, try someone else. Just talking about how you got to this point in your life can release a lot of the pressure that's building up and help you find a way to cope.

Bullied Back to Life

# Chapter 5

# Prison Without Bars*: Graham Swann's story

Swanny walked into McDonald's in Loughborough to meet up with me for a coffee. I wanted to know more about the man I'd listened to during a church service two weeks earlier. My wife and I had been invited by our friends, Matt and Hannah, who had organised Swanny's visit to a church we used to attend. We knew enough about the man to fix the date firmly in our diary. We didn't want to miss listening to what we felt would be a moving and emotional testimony, and we weren't disappointed.

Swanny, real name Graham Swann, held us both, and the 100 or so other people he addressed, in the palm of his hand. His highly personal account of his subjection to physical bullying was just the start; it got a whole lot more brutal and heart-breaking thereafter, at least until the twist came and the light began to dawn. Swanny spilled out details of the violence he'd endured, and even more shockingly, later administered, and his subsequent regret and shame. Swanny's talk was emotionally super-charged and sad, really sad, but I will save you the detail and leave it to the man himself to explain it all later on. Swanny has written a book about it all, *Prison Without Bars*, and his account below is a taster of what the book contains. If his story here interests you, then I'd strongly recommend that you obtain a copy of his book, which is available in paperback and on Kindle.

Him mentioning the violence he dished back out really surprised me; it was a curve ball thrown in I didn't see coming. The man from the council estates of Shelthorpe in Loughborough explained with enough detail for us to get more than a snapshot, how he was subjected to the most violent acts of bullying imaginable. The revelation then followed how he'd turned against those who had subjected him to such torture and basically anyone who he didn't like the look of.

* Excerpted from *Prison Without Bars: A journey from brokenness to wholeness; from hopelessness to hope*

He became the bully, and his accounts of that transformation didn't make for easy listening. His wife Rachel was sat in front of him and I couldn't help noticing their strong connection. Perhaps it was those looks he sent her way when he ventured into the darker corners of his life, and how she seemed to reassure him just by her presence. They had gone through this together and relived it all hundreds of times over, having visited church after church to bring their message of hope, when all had seemed dark and too broken to fix.

The day after I heard Swanny's story I drove to his tattoo shop to hand him the outline details of my new book and a copy of the one I have written, with a Post-It note on it. The note politely asked him to read the opening chapter, which gave details of my own experiences of being bullied. I wanted him to get a sense of my pain before hoping he would be moved enough to agree to telling his own story in my book. His shop was closed so I pushed it through the letter box. A few emails were exchanged and eventually the meeting was on.

McDonald's was my choice of venue because it was smack opposite Swanny's tattoo shop, and I didn't want to inconvenience him by dragging him too far away from his own location. After all, I was the one who initiated this meeting, with my mission very clear, which was basically to get him to produce a chapter for this book, and I wanted as much time with him as possible.

The moment Swanny walked in, heads turned his way, maybe because he had tattoos all over his arms and neck, and the fact that his shaven head made him look lean and mean. Or it might have been due to the fact that all the staff knew him, together with one or two customers or a combination of those possibilities. Then a warm smile filled his face as he greeted me as I walked over to say hello, and I couldn't help feeling immediately relaxed and ready for our chat. By his own admission, Swanny isn't the tallest. That's part of the reason why the start of his story has included so much heartache and pain – he was picked on and maliciously bullied as a child, and that was only the start of his bumpy ride.

Some pleasantries were exchanged before I confessed that I was happy I hadn't met him some 30 or so years ago. That was the time he ruled over Shelthorpe with terror, hatred and physical aggression. Swanny smiled at my comment and told me that many people have said the same thing.

This intriguing and warm human being seated opposite me drinking his cappuccino was anything but the man who raised hell back in the day; in fact you could say he was the complete opposite now. He'd turned to God, which was his only path to redemption and a way of saving him from the self-loathing, shame and regret he'd been burdened with for over 30 years. He was tired of feeling unworthy of any kind of happiness. Drugs and alcohol had fed his hate-filled being for far too long.

Before you begin to formulate any kind of opinion of someone caught up in so much violence, reserve judgment until you hear his story. It's heartfelt and incredibly honest and then hopefully you will begin to understand why it all unravelled for Swanny in the way that it did.

He has been victim AND villain, bullied AND bully. I had been looking for someone who had seen both sides of that coin. His harrowing account of torture he endured from other boys at his school sets up what was to follow. You can soon see where his motivation to dish out violence came from! It helps to explain, although certainly not excuse, exactly why someone could victimise, threaten and beat innocent people. I needed to look this man in the eye and explore beneath the surface. Swanny was incredibly open and sensitive to a past he isn't proud of, yet he believes he was saved by something which every person who knew him found difficult at first to comprehend.

This amazing man runs a soup kitchen for the homeless and the lost. He also visits prisons to speak to the hearts of those as troubled as he was. He visits Uganda to help the poor and oppressed and he gives his time and money to help in whichever way he can.

"Saved by Jesus," was a phrase Swanny has used after explaining calmly the violence, terror and heartbreak that had cursed his life before those words were first spoken. He left no stone unturned as he opened the lid to his life.

A few minutes into our conversation a McDonald's staff member politely intervened to mention something about a knife attack that had happened in Loughborough the night before; Swanny was clearly upset. He told her that it's such a problem – kids carrying knives not because they want to attack but in case they are attacked. It's like it has become a mandatory thing to carry a weapon. He appeared to understand the mindset of those caught up in these crimes. His knowledge and experience gave both of us a better understanding and less of a judgmental attitude. Swanny believes in forgiveness; he's the guy in the corner of the outlaw and the outcast, and he's the guy who draws alongside the victims of today, based on his own mistakes and negative experiences. There is no one who understands more about all this than this man!

I told Swanny I wanted to protect him from any kickback if he felt he was comfortable in sharing his story. The purpose of including his story is to help people to understand the strength needed to turn our lives around, no matter what it has entailed or whatever may lie in our past.

I feel a responsibility to all our contributors of stories, as they are laying bare difficult events in their lives, and I fear that some might not fully understand or sympathise with some of us. A wry smile from Swanny said it all. I realised that he, of anyone, didn't need protection but he politely nodded anyway and appreciated my concern.

As a fellow Christian I can't and won't judge Swanny, as he himself won't judge me or anyone else for that matter. He knows how his past has hurt others, and still continues to hurt some of those people today. He is also well aware that the focus on his faith causes some raised eyebrows regarding its authenticity.

I was left feeling impressed with and inspired by this warm human being who not only faces up to his past, but who also refuses to forget it... and more importantly how he uses it to change people's lives today. It's what he spends his life doing now that leaves me with feelings of respect and admiration. He's a shining light to his church family and the Shelthorpe community, who hold him in high regard despite his past.

After our time together, it felt like we had known each other for much more than an hour and a half and before we went our separate ways he embraced me with a compassionate hug, like a brother, and I couldn't help feeling we would share a few more coffees moving forward.

# Here is Swanny's story...

## Prologue

We were sitting in a park on a swelteringly hot summer's day. It was just Rachel, me and a specially prepared picnic. Viewed from the outside it seemed like an idyllic setting, some quality time with the woman I loved. But this superficial veneer masked a world of inner torture and turmoil.

To date my life had not so much been a journey, but rather a series of collisions and crashes. Occasional highs were wiped out by crushing lows. Childhood trauma had set the stage for a dysfunctional adult life that could never be put right without divine intervention. I had thrown myself into jobs, drink and even crime to try to forget the pain and hurt of the past, but I couldn't forget. No matter what I did, I couldn't shake off my past.

The child I had been haunted the man I had become. This lost boy followed me doggedly, constantly speaking the same words to me, over and over again: "Don't tell – it's our secret. Don't be weak, Swanny."

"Why won't you leave me alone!" my head screamed. I wanted to talk, to tell Rachel the truth, to just let it all come spilling out, but the words died in my throat. "Keep the secret, Swanny. Don't tell..." As quickly and easily as the intimacy between us blossomed, I felt myself pushing Rachel away. I was about to ruin a perfect afternoon... again.

## A shadow is cast

A shadow was cast over the sunny, happy days of my childhood when I was about 10 years old. Things changed for everybody, including me, and not for the better. My brother, Tony, began to bring distress and anxiety into the family. He was always fighting and beginning to get into trouble breaking into properties.

The effect this had on mam and dad was both immense and very obvious to me. "Your dad's had a breakdown", mam sobbed, her tears flowing freely, the corners of her mouth quivering with emotion. He was wandering around like a lost soul, shaven-headed, staring at the ground.

Life was never the same again. Dad never really recovered and Tony continually brought aggravation home. Alongside a dawning reality that my former safe, secure, family environment was crumbling, I was being bullied. It had started a couple of months earlier. Maybe I would have spoken up about it in different circumstances. But because of the turmoil at home, where everyone was consumed by their own problems, I stayed silent. The feelings of insecurity I felt were surfacing at school and the other kids had begun to pick up on it. I became vulnerable, a target for those who were inclined to be hurtful and unkind. Soon I became the headline attraction for the warped amusement of others.

At first it was shoving, needless confrontation, the odd punch in the face; eventually it was just sheer evil. I was beaten on a daily basis and forced to hand over my pocket money.

I was small for my age and skinny. Frail in body, but now in mind too. The bullies robbed me of the last vestiges of my self-confidence. The bullies abused not just my body, but my mind. Frequently I was ordered to strip down to my pants and run. I was given a head start and then hunted down like a fox. When I was caught I was thrashed with branches; hounded like prey and then whipped.

One particular day began like so many others. The gang of bullies was on my tail once again and I had been pursued like a dog across some fields. But after the expected beating and kicking they had devised a new form of sick punishment. They dragged me to a spot in the field they'd discovered where there was something resembling a crater in the ground. It was a large hole, filled with manure.

It was the height of summer and the sun's rays had baked a hardened crust over the top of this pit. Underneath it would be like coagulated syrup. The lads thought it would provide some great entertainment for them if I was forced to walk across the crust, to see if it would bear my weight.

I'd only taken a few steps when my shoes began to stick and the crust groaned and shifted. My progress became laboured and I began to be sucked down, my legs fighting helplessly against the viscous treacle. Every movement I made worsened my situation and the more I struggled the more I was eaten up by the pit. I had reached the point where the possibility of being completely sucked under was very real. I was minutes away from inevitable suffocation. Time stood still as the realisation hit home. The yelling and laughter was abruptly terminated and I could see the expressions of terror on the gang's faces, mirroring my own. "Help!" I screamed. But no one helped. No one wanted to be implicated in the tragedy of another boy's death. Like the pathetic, weak bullies they were, every last one turned and ran, leaving me to my fate.

I gave out one last desperate scream for help and was amazed to find a strong hand grabbing the scruff of my neck. The farmer whose field it was happened to be nearby and came to investigate the noise. He saved my life – but he didn't do so cheerfully. After dragging me out of the pit he ordered me to get off his land and added that he'd take a pot shot at me with his gun if I ever trespassed again.

I began to really hate my life. I felt alone, afraid, isolated and abandoned. I genuinely believed that no one loved me – not even my family. I felt as though I was merely surviving life; unaccompanied, unsupported and unloved.

I also began to follow in Tony's footsteps and started getting into problems at school as my troubled existence began to spill over into other areas of my life. Mam was constantly being called in to see one of my teachers or the headmaster. I think the teachers got bored with trying to whack some sense into me with a plimsoll. To me it was nothing compared with the beatings I was receiving outside of school.

One day, I began my usual dash, across the playground and out of the gates as fast as my skinny legs would carry me. All the time I was looking over my shoulder, afraid that the bullies were onto me. I was nearly home, when I heard a gruff voice calling to me. "Oi! What are you looking at?" I looked around and there he was, an ugly giant of a man with bulging eyes standing in the doorway to his house. For some reason his stare arrested my progress and I felt glued to the spot. After what seemed like a long time I spoke in a trembling voice: "Nothing."

"Come here", he ordered. His face was expressionless.

I didn't speak, but I shook my head.

'Come here", he said again, voice softening slightly. I shook my head, but he persisted.

"Come here, I want to show you something."

I don't know why, but I felt as though he had some power over me. I didn't want to see whatever it was he wanted to show me; I didn't want to go into his house. Yet I made my way tentatively down his path. He towered over me, a monstrous figure, eclipsing me. "Come on lad, hurry up," he said and seconds later I was stepping into his house for the first time.

# The tide turns

I had become the prey of a predatory paedophile; a victim of sexual abuse. There are no words to describe how I felt as I walked away from my abuser's house. One minute I was sprinting home, pleased to have evaded capture for once, the next I was caught in a new trap. My life changed forever that day.

My captor instructed me to go upstairs and ordered me to lie on his bed and close my eyes. I was so terrified that fear immobilised me. I couldn't move. He put a pillow over my head and I just lay there like a corpse until he had finished using me. I wanted my mam to come and save me, but I knew I was alone, helpless to stop it.

My abuser had something in common with my bullies. He'd chanced his arm to try and exploit me and had immediately seen my weakness and vulnerability. He must have been delighted that I didn't have the self-confidence to resist him. Every beating I received and every touch from the hands of this pervert drove me deeper within myself until I became the lost boy who was destined to haunt the grown man.

My abuser controlled me by destroying every last shred of self-worth. He played his power game with me every day. He said he would kill me if I didn't do what he wanted or if I dared to tell anyone.

Some reading this might think, why didn't you stop it? Why didn't you avoid this man, run away, tell someone what was happening? The truth is, I felt absolutely powerless to do anything, such was my lack of self-worth and self-confidence. I was vulnerable, exposed, and so low and desperate that these people succeeded in exerting their wills upon me and I just crumbled and gave in. I was only 10-years old. I didn't know what to do.

After three years of abuse I was an emotional husk. On the outside I looked like any other kid entering his teens, but on the inside there was nothing. I was dead behind the eyes. Day in and day out I was molested by a faceless beast who only cared about one thing, his perverted self-gratification. Three and a bit years... that man abused me over a thousand times. To me it felt like a thousand lifetimes.

Later, as reaching my teens ushered in a move to a new school and a new routine, I would eventually escape his clutches. But after three years of abuse, he had inflicted a lifetime's emotional damage. The physical abuse may have ended, but his control over my mind and emotions would hold me captive for years to come.

During my early years at Garendon High School I was still being bullied in school and abused out of it. I was a shadow; an isolated, troubled kid. But there came a certain day at Garendon when everything changed and my life took a new direction. From nowhere a single incident caused a change of perspective and the tide turned. Here's how it unfolded:

One of my long-time bullies had cornered me, just me and him. The physical abuse started on its normal escalating scale, culminating in him pummelling my face with a volley of punches. Quite suddenly a bigger, older lad appeared – someone I knew from down the street. Without hesitation he confronted the bully. "Oi!" he shouted, "try throwing that same punch at me." The bully froze with fear; immobilised. I couldn't believe what I was seeing. I read the same terror in him that had been familiar to me for so long.

It was as though someone had reached inside me and flicked off the "victim" switch. I was euphoric. For the first time in living memory I experienced the feeling of power. And I loved it. I was used to being the victim, the bullied, the abused. In a second all that had changed.

From that day on, from somewhere, I don't know where, I found a new determination. No one was ever going to touch me again – no bully, no sexual abuser – and it felt amazing. From that day forward, not a single person bothered me again. But at what cost? I had been beaten down, bullied, abused and oppressed for years, but though I was no longer a victim, I'd crossed over to the dark side. I had become an aggressor. I was set to become the one thing that I had despised for so long: a bully.

The change in my character was rapid and spread like an uncontrollable rash. I became no better than my tormentors. And yet, it was addictive. I was able to dominate those who were helpless and I'd be lying if I said I didn't enjoy it for all it was worth. I learnt to swagger around, an arrogant kid, giving everyone the evil eye. I respected no one and cared little if I lived or died. Gone was the carefree kid; gone was the bullied kid. Here came the cheerless, stone-hearted, violent monster.

## A chance to change

Over time, I moved far beyond simply sticking up for myself, getting into fights on the basis of self-defence. I relished violence. I enjoyed inflicting pain on others. I was still a teenager, but I had the mind of a fighter double my age. I was getting physically stronger all the time, but I was also fuelled by anger, resentment and bitterness.

The next few years, therefore, sailed by on a tide of violence. I was like a magnet who pulled other, like-minded, kids towards me. We were attracted to one another; we dealt with life in a similar way. Eventually my schooling reached its own conclusion when I was expelled. My relationship with education was over.

The streets taught me to trust no one. This may have worked on the streets, but it made it nigh on impossible for me to develop any kind of normal relationship with anyone. This became very evident the day I met Lesley. She was a whole three years older than me and that made me feel kind of cool. Lesley cared for me but I repaid her care with paranoia. I was full of mistrust for this girl. I pushed her away at every opportunity, yet when she pushed me away in return, I just turned my back. My emotional barricade was far too extreme to be penetrated.

I was dangerous for two reasons. One, I didn't care who I fought and never considered whether I could beat them or not, and second, I had no sympathy for anyone. After I'd beaten someone to a pulp, I didn't feel a thing – or at least not until the red mist had subsided, which took a very long time. Only then did I feel even a twinge of remorse.

One day when I was with Lesley she dropped the bombshell on me that she was pregnant. I was just 17 and deeply troubled; now I was going to be a dad. I was struggling to deal with myself, so I couldn't imagine how I would manage with a baby. Nevertheless, I decided I should move in with Lesley and give this a go. I left my mam and dad's and set up home as a so-called grown up.

My daughter was born in the April of 1984. I was on cloud nine. She was precious, cherished; I loved her more than anything else.

I tried my best to be good enough, but my past overwhelmed me. People had had enough of me – my parents, the police, society, it felt like. I was constantly in serious trouble. Meanwhile, I was father to a perfect, innocent little girl and busy trying to kid myself into believing life was good. It was a lie. I failed Lesley and my little girl with my false promises. It wasn't long before the police were knocking on my door. I was hauled up before a judge. Within hours I would be on my way to a new home; one which consisted of three meals a day, scrubbing floors and fighting to survive – prison.

## Broken promises

As the judge passed sentence my heart sank into the depths of despair. The long list of misdemeanours I'd committed flashed before my eyes: endless brutality, muggings, robberies. That moment the judge passed sentence on me I was struck by the sinking sense that I had thrown away everything I cherished. I was about to be locked up and, although it wasn't a high security prison, it was a secure unit and I was being deprived of my freedom. I felt very isolated.

At night, when all was silent, I would wrestle with my thoughts and emotions. I grieved the loss of my freedom. I indulged in self-pity. Despite this, my aggression grew thicker, like weeds in an untended garden, suffocating every other emotion. Being locked away was supposed to be teaching me a lesson, but instead it was fuelling my anger.

All things pass and, in due course, I was released to resume my life. I got it into my head that perhaps things would improve if I married Lesley. I thought that having a wife and a baby, having a proper home, would somehow change everything for the better. So, Lesley and I married but, of course, I was wrong. It wasn't that simple. I was still the same person inside.

The day my son was born was such a perfect one for me. I was so pleased. Now I had one of each – who could ask for more? But Lesley and I continued to damage one another. We would argue over anything and everything. Instead of life getting better it continued as before. The police were never far from our door and I believed what everyone said about me: I was a fool and a trouble-maker who'd sooner smash someone with a baseball bat than shake their hand. I was a waste of space; no use to anyone.

## What if's

I had to go. I had to say goodbye. Although I hated the expected consequences of leaving my kids, in the end I felt it would be better for them if I wasn't there. The separation was tough and leaving my children was heart-breaking. I was a screwed up 26-year-old when I took the decision to walk away.

Being apart from my kids was the toughest fight I'd ever known. But in some strange way it became a catalyst for me. It ignited a small spark within me – a resolve that somehow I must change my life.

## A gap in the clouds

The passage of time and prolonged separation had taken its course. Lesley and I were now divorced. Things just didn't work when we were together. We had no future. So what now?

On a night out, my mate spotted a couple of girls on the other side of the pub and wanted me to go over with him to start a conversation. We made our way over. I'd seen one of the girls – the one I liked – around the Shelthorpe area from time to time. Normally I would never have made the first move to speak, but with a few beers inside me I thought, why not?

"Hello, what's your name then?" I asked, the drink giving me a false self-confidence. I looked at her and couldn't help grinning like an idiot. She looked stunning. My heart raced and I felt nervous – that rush of adrenalin you feel when you really like someone. I'd never known anything like it.

"My name's Rachel, what's yours?"

What followed was a courtship entered into by Rachel with some caution, given my local reputation.

Rachel decided to give it a go with me. She thought I was worth the risk. She said that behind all my tattoos she could see a really nice person. "You don't have to control your life with your fist," she told me. "You should use your heart. It's love that makes the world go round, Swanny."

In time, Rachel and I were married. What followed were some great times – holidays away as a family, seeing the kids grow up and making our home just the way we wanted it to be. Life was good. We made the best of it. Then, in 1996, we decided to have our own baby together. I was so proud of Rachel the day our little boy was born. All our kids were special to us and we loved them all to bits. But having our own son was the icing on the cake and completed our family.

Viewed from the outside my life looked good. But inside me it was a different story. I was unable to get over my secret past. It was always there to haunt me and rob me of enjoying all these good things. The only way out of this nightmare was, I thought, to drink myself into oblivion.

Ultimately, the drink never did help. Still, in the dead of night, the lost boy would come and visit me, trying to persuade me to keep all of this locked up inside when I wanted so badly to let it all out. All I wanted was to tell Rachel the truth. How could I find a way?

## Light breaks through

Though life had improved dramatically and I had much to be grateful for, I was still an emotional prisoner. I wanted nothing more than to spill my guts and let the ugly truth out – to tell the person I loved most what I had been through. But at the same time, the thought of doing so terrified me. It meant that, for the first time, I'd have to let my guard down and become completely vulnerable – something I had trained myself not to do. Plus, it was hard enough coping with the truth myself; how would I cope with someone else knowing my inner torment? Scared to let go, I decided to suffer in silence and carry on the act.

In the summer of 2006, however, another chance meeting caused a new twist in my journey. I have a good friend Steve, whose sister, Louise, married an American called Tyler. They lived in Florida for a while, but in 2006, they moved back to the UK. Had they not, my life might have turned out differently.

Tyler had given up a fantastic career and a guaranteed pension to come and live in England, in Loughborough, and one day in the local pub I asked him why he had made that decision.

"God told me to," he replied matter-of-factly.

I almost choked on my beer. He'd said it like it was the most natural thing in the world.

"What are you on about?" I said, laughing in his face. "You mean your instincts told you to?"

"No buddy, I mean God told me to."

He went on to explain that he was a Christian. I thought he was completely nuts. But despite what I saw as Tyler's crackpot beliefs, our friendship deepened. As time went on, I listened to Tyler speak about God on many occasions.

To read in full about the path my life next took, then please read my book *Prison Without Bars*. But suffice to say, I asked God to come into my life. I asked Him to forgive me for all the things I'd done wrong and to help me with the problems I'd carried with me for so many years. More waves of overwhelming love swept over me and I knew... I was free at last.

God Bless you,
*Swanny.*

**What an amazing story of victimhood, of being the bully and of redemption!**

If you have been moved and inspired by Swanny's story, as I was, then the part of it that Swanny has kindly agreed that we can reproduce here is just a part of his journey. You can read the whole story in his fantastic book, *Prison Without Bars*, which is available in paperback or as a Kindle book. Highly recommended reading!

I have mentioned that this is a book not only for those who have suffered the effects of bullying, but also for those who are currently demonstrating bullying behaviour or are guilty of having bullied at least one person in the past. **Might this describe you?**

Before feeling challenged and put on the spot, here's an interesting statistic for you. A charity which supports victims of bullying, Ditch the Label, reported in their 2015 survey that **50% of young people have bullied someone else.**

It's never too late to stop! Whether you're guilty of some form of past bullying or caught up in it now. It's what happens next that counts, as we can learn from Swanny's story.

I never expected to meet up with someone who would openly admit to bullying others, and Swanny gave me and hopefully you a vivid insight into why he embarked on this path. And whether you believe in God or not, there's plenty in this story for us all to learn from as to why someone might turn to bullying.

I took from this story that, at least initially, Swanny hit out at anyone he saw as a threat, borne out of his fear of being physically attacked and sexually abused himself. That was his defence mechanism after being the victim for so long. The sad twist came with the shift of power he felt as he turned his attention onto almost anyone, even those who had done him no harm.

And then, after all the pain and hurt he had caused, the guilt, the regret, and then the redemption!

To most of the world, including all those people he targeted and victimised, Swanny would have been written off a long time ago. But look at his turnaround, surely that is to be respected, if not admired!

> **❝ People who love themselves, ❞
> don't hurt other people. The
> more we hate ourselves, the
> more we want others to suffer.**
>
> — Dan Pearce

There's a well-known verse in the Bible that says, "Let him who is without sin cast the first stone" (John 8, verse 7.) It refers to a woman who people wanted to stone to death and punish for committing adultery. Jesus tells them that the person who has no sins should be the first to throw a stone. Of course, everyone has sinned, so no one can throw any stones. I think this verse in poignant and relatable, certainly in Swanny's case, and in my own too. No one is devoid of wrongdoing and everyone should have a chance to wipe the slate clean and start again, otherwise what is the point?

If you were to have met me when I was 18, I know most of you wouldn't have taken to me; I didn't even like myself. So how could I expect someone else to respect who I was? Fast forward over 30 years and I am a different version of me.

I don't think Swanny, for one moment, is asking for our forgiveness; he has sought this from a higher source. Whether some of us can fully believe or comprehend that or not, you've got to at least look at how he lives his life now.

For the all the wrong this man has done, let's remember, he's had unimaginable wrong done to him, and before you begin to judge, he is the first to admit that this simply doesn't excuse any of the bad stuff he's dished out.

Having spent time with Swanny, I can see that he refuses to spend the rest of his life apologising for and regretting part of his past, when he can instead use it as a positive force for good by moving forward and helping others.

Ray Dawson, whose story is included earlier, unearthed a simple explanation as to why someone might bully another person. "Because I could", was the simple answer he received when asking two of his own bullies why they made his life hell. Such an arrogant yet honest reply, but so true. These bullies felt they could victimise someone simply because they realised that their victims were weaker than them.

Here's another answer to the same question, WHY? That was put to a former bully, who chose anonymity in an article by Telegraph journalist, Angus Watson, published in 2004.

"There was one boy, Edmund Jones, who had giant ears, yellow skin, smelt of urine and whose father was the mild-mannered French teacher. Unfortunately, because of this cruel combination of circumstances, he got it.

One day, Bill Davis, my impressive friend from the year above, came into our classroom. There were three of us there, and Jones.

"What are you doing?" Davis asked.

"We're trying to make Jones cry just by teasing him." I answered.

"That's not how to make Jones cry," he replied, picking up Jones's cheap, heavy briefcase. He ran around all the desks gathering speed and stopped just before Jones and let go of the case. It hit Jones in the midriff like a battering ram and burst open in an explosion of paper, books, conkers and sweet wrappers.

"That's how you make Jones cry," said Davis as Jones ran from the room sobbing.

I was awed by Davis's style and inventiveness. From that day, I raised my game. Bullying took on a crueller and more imaginative twist. Breaking expensive Caran d'Ache pencils while their owners watched, teasing them about their mothers' hairstyles, throwing sticks dipped in sheep-poo at them, and so on. Pretty horrible stuff, and certainly nothing to remember with pride. So why did I do it?

Other than the fact that I was plain nasty, it was part of my childhood culture. My big brother whacked me with happy regularity, as did all my dormitory captains at boarding school. One particular prefect would make us drink water until we were sick. Another made my friend cut me with an army tin opener.

My friends and I used to stab each other, and ourselves, with compasses for amusement. We used to spray deodorant from very close on to our skin, making it blister. I still have scars from that. Pain was all around. Bullying, I suppose, was a way of passing this on to the weaker boys."

Honest and revealing accounts of a former school bully, who admittedly switched off from bullying when, at 12, he "discovered girls."

Bullying behaviour doesn't have to be so pre-planned and callously executed.

What about random acts of bullying, something we might feel is harmless banter?

Could this mean me or you? Absolutely it could, and probably does. For sure, I've been in a group of people where someone has latched onto something that I have said or done that makes everyone else laugh. And I've been only too happy to have chipped in when the attention falls on someone else's shoulders, giving me some much-needed respite. Is this just banter? Yes, it could be, and for sure it mostly is (I think) but there is a fine line that can be easily crossed without us even being conscious of it happening.

If we are honest you could argue that, quite often, someone walks away hurt by random comments spoken "in jest."

What is the word jest meant to mean anyway, because people tend to tell the truth when they "jest" don't they? And because you might say to that person when they are on their own, looking hurt, "Sorry about jesting with you earlier," doesn't take away from the fact that they clearly think that you and your friends think that they are a bit dull, or have a big nose, or wear bad clothes, or whatever that personal jest included, does it?

Sounds a bit harsh when I insinuate that we like hunting in packs, but it's often true!

We all need to check ourselves and take responsibility for our words, or our silence as a bystander if we witness verbal attacks against others. Banter is harmless until it gets too personal.

I am sure we can all point to some comment that has cut us to our core, or remember back, if we care to, to some loaded comment we fired off that we know caused some emotional damage to another person.

Certainly, in writing this book and doing all the research, I have become much more self-aware of these situations; I can only hope you are beginning to feel the same.

And finally, I found this useful information on the BulliesOut website...

# Are you bullying someone?

Recognising bullying behaviour in others is quite easy but are we able to see those behaviours in ourselves? It can be difficult to look at our own behaviour because we might find something we don't like or we know is not acceptable – something like bullying.

Bullying is NOT a laugh or a joke. Bullying is cruel and has a devastating effect on all involved and can ruin people's lives.

The comments below are from young people who have completed our questionnaire. Their names have been changed to protect their identities. If you think bullying is OK or a joke, then maybe these comments will make you realise it isn't.

"I can't take anymore. I just want it to stop." Lucy, 14

"He kept on and on and on. The punches weren't so bad. It was the comments that hurt more." Tom, 16

"I don't want to go to school anymore. They make my life hell. No-one listens. I want to end it all." Ray, 14

"As a result of bullying, I developed an eating disorder at 13 which lasted until I was in my mid-thirties. I've never really got over it." Ann, 54

Bullying creates a culture of fear and has a negative impact on everyone involved. Being bullied can seriously affect a person's physical, emotional, academic and social well-being. Many sufferers of bullying lack confidence, feel bad about themselves, have few friends and spend a lot of time alone. If you are bullying somebody, is this how you really want to make them feel?

# Why do people bully?

According to research from ditchthelabel.org most people bully because they are looking to gain a feeling of power, purpose and control over another person. Of course, there are other reasons too:

To gain attention

To take things from someone

They might be jealous of the person they are bullying

They may be feeling unhappy and/or insecure

They may have been bullied themselves

They're using bullying as a defence mechanism – by bullying others, they're immune to being bullied themselves

They have low self-esteem

They have a difficult home life

Sometimes, a person is displaying bullying behaviour and does not realise they're doing it or the effects it is having on others

Whilst this doesn't condone what they do, understanding what might be behind a bully's behaviour can sometimes help the situation and ensure they receive the relevant help and support needed to encourage them to change their behaviour.

Bullying is like an addiction and bullies can become addicted to the power and control they have over others.

## Chapter 6

# Fanning the Flame of Good: Thomas Dahlborg's story

In preparing this book I dug deep to find a selection of personal stories that would represent a diverse range of bullying experiences, but I didn't expect to come across examples of a parent and child working as a team, to combat its effect.

My Google research had led me to a story that had unfolded across the Atlantic where there are some obvious cultural differences compared to what I have experienced in the UK.

However, the way bullies operate is the same; they all demonstrate behavioural traits common throughout mankind.

I had come across some articles written by an American named Thomas H Dahlborg, who is a massive influencer in US healthcare. I was drawn to his incredible use of words, his intelligence, his sense of integrity and most of all his undeniable love for his son, who suffered mental and emotional bullying primarily by adults. He writes about how, through Tommy playing basketball, with his help and support in his roles as both father and basketball coach, his son Tommy has been able to develop a degree of resilience which has sustained him to this day.

Thomas H Dahlborg inspired me enough to call him and by the end of our 30-minute chat he was just Tom, a warm and lovely father to his amazing son Tommy, and his genuine character and kindness matched the words he'd written. I was so humbled by what he shared with me.

Tom had a story to tell, actually he'd already written about it, and authored a book, which chronicled how he helped Tommy work through sport-based bullying, stemming from his coaches who told him he was "too big and too slow to participate." The book, *The Big Kid and Basketball... and the Lessons he Taught His Father and Coach* demonstrates something that intrigued me, something I'd never experienced myself (not to this degree, anyway) or really thought too much about. It reveals with heartfelt compassion how a parent takes on the responsibility because of a flawed coaching system, to help their child overcome bullying tactics, sometimes subtle, but nonetheless very divisive.

During my own childhood in the 60s and 70s, relying on my parents to help me wasn't an option. There just wasn't a culture of seeking and finding support from any adults. I think this was a common scenario back then, and every era before that. Children affected by bullying soon learned that they basically had to keep tight-lipped as, and I know this from my own experience, it was seen as an act of cowardice to tell a teacher or a parent. The bullies seemed to dictate the terms of all stages of their actions and how we, on the receiving end, were meant to deal with the aftermath.

Occasionally, as my own personal experiences show, and also those of many people of around my age I have spoken to since, teachers themselves resorted to acts of violence as a way of keeping order in the classroom.

In my secondary school it wasn't uncommon for a pupil to be slapped around their head or grabbed by their lapels and either rigorously shaken, or in some instances thrown to the floor. It happened to me and I even felt I deserved the occasional caning I got from my headmaster as a final consequence of my immature behaviour. He would never have thought for one moment to look deeper into why I behaved in the way I did. To be fair to him, there simply wasn't any mechanism in place or the time required to offer and execute the support "troubled" pupils like me might have required.

The punishment was often an instant reaction to a behavioural issue and therefore swift in its administration; no wonder we kept our shame to ourselves.

With so-called role models of teachers (and of course more than a few parents too) demonstrating that it was OK to subject individuals weaker than themselves, their pupils, to habitual and casual acts of violence, no wonder bullies thrived and the bullied suffered in silence. Certainly, within schools, the culture has thankfully moved on from acts of institutional bullying (because that is what is was) being in any way acceptable.

> **66 Knowing what's right doesn't 99 mean much unless you do what's right. School administrators can't say it's up to the parents. Parents can't say it's up to the teachers. Teachers can't say it's not their job. And kids can't say, "I was too afraid to tell." Every single one of us has to play our role if we're serious about putting an end to the madness. We are all responsible. We must be.**
>
> — Megan Kelley Hall

Tommy was a representative of a generation after my era and although he didn't face the same type of problems I had come up against, what he went through wasn't any less destructive to his own mind. The negative forces at his school, in his chosen sport environment, and via other parents, conspired against him. No, not in a physical way – comments and whispers were often cleverly indirect yet devastatingly corrosive and damaging to a young boy's confidence.

His father, Tom, could have flipped, who would have blamed him? However, he isn't that type of human being, and chose instead to draw alongside his son to look at and work around it from a completely different angle.

I have read Tom's book and it touched my heart. I felt the pain Tommy had felt because I was a bigger schoolboy too and I know how it felt to be disowned, ignored and excluded from peer groups for being "different."

I would recommend that you read Tom's fascinating and inspirational book – it's cleverly written, extremely humorous and sad in equal measures.

The same problem plagued me yet again, as with some other story contributors... that of finding a way, in this written piece, for Tom to open up his and Tommy's story beyond what was already documented in his own book. I needed more for it to fit the narrative of my own book.

I had presumed that being big meant that Tommy was extremely tall for his age, so quite innocently I asked Tom, via email, what his height was, as I couldn't find it in his book.

I also asked for more specifics in relation to the bullying Tommy had endured.

Tom's email came back a few days later than I had expected, and I began to think I had pushed too far and upset him.

In the most eloquent manner, Tom put me in my place by suggesting I had missed the point. He didn't exactly say that, but I sensed it in his words. Here's part of what he typed, "My son was deemed to be too fat, that's what I mean when I describe him as big." Then the penny began to drop as he continued...

"What happened to Tommy in basketball and my intent to share it was to highlight how he developed resilience to withstand challenges thrown at him, NOT to focus more attention on the bullying behaviour of a coach."

It suddenly dawned on me – his story didn't need the detail; it was clear what was happening without opening it up all up to the degree I had requested. The word "big" could be exchanged for anything the world can't deal with unless it's through humour or sarcasm, and the book speaks for those people who stand out in this way.

> **❝ If they don't like you for being ❞ yourself, be yourself even more.**
>
> — Taylor Swift

Over the phone, Tom made clear his feelings about how a subtle form of continuous bullying had devastated his son as much as any form of bullying could affect anyone, and it all made sense.

I know what exclusion feels like; it's happened to me, in the playground, for being uniquely different. It's also happened to me in the business world for the same reason. It's a lonely path to have to tread, and yes, most of it stems from things being said that are subtle!

Ok, point definitely taken and understood from my side. Tom was right, his integrity shone through, and he did tailor their story accordingly. I was however mindful that this book is also about the wins readers might gain from these personal stories of adversity. Also, what positive inspiration we might pass on to others who find themselves in similar positions to us, and Tom obliged with how they both work with the oppressed and abused.

Sometimes the scars can appear to be too deep to fully heal, even many years after the act of bullying has ceased, but the success of overcoming hurdles and inspiring others who suffer must bring some justification for the suffering. With that in mind here is Tom

& Tommy's story, preceded firstly by the "professional description of Thomas":

Thomas H. Dahlborg is an industry voice for Relationship Centered and Compassionate Care AND Servant and Relationship Centered Leadership.

An author, consultant and advisor, he is also a nationally recognized speaker, partner and collaborator. He is passionate about changing the healthcare system to a healthCARING system.

Tom has more than 30 years of extensive leadership experience building relationship centered, patient-and-family focused, empathetic, compassionate care models; analyzing and meeting patient and family expectations; optimizing strategic partnerships, ventures and teams; innovating leadership, and bending the cost curve.

# Here's Tom & Tommy's story

### Fanning the Flame of Good[1]

27% of children report being bullied by parents.

"Mommy. Daddy. All the kids are next door. Can I go over and play too?"

Tommy, our son who was about 5 years old at the time, had several friends his age in the neighbourhood. Brendon, Tommy's best friend, lived next door.

Of course, you can go play, Tommy, my wife and I replied.

And as we kissed Tommy prior to his departure, we noticed his beautiful smile, the one deep dimple on the right side of his face, and his glistening blue eyes. Our boy. Our boy, who was born beautiful ... and with neurological challenges. Yes, our boy we were sending off to explore and to be with his friends.

"Have fun, T. Love you."

"Love you too, Dad."

Now, Tommy didn't just walk across our side yard and up to the door of our neighbor's home ... he skipped. He skipped with his slight leftward lean and awkward gait and yet he skipped with the

---

1 *Excerpted from The Big Kid and Basketball ... and the lessons he taught his Father and Coach*

glee of a young child about to be with those who know only love ... children. And at that, the unconditional love of friendship.

Three minutes later ...

"Mommy! Daddy! Why? Why can't I play with my friends? What did Brendon's mother mean? Please. Please. I want to play with my friends. Why?! What does she mean? Why can't I play?" Tommy wailed as tears poured down his cheeks.

"Tommy, what happened? What did Mrs. Williams say to you?"

"Brendon's mother, she said, she said, mom, dad, she said, she yelled, 'Tommy, you are *too big* to come in and play. Go home!'"

42% of children report being bullied by physical education teachers and coaches.

During the summer between Tommy's sophomore and junior year in High School, when he was 16, Tommy played what is known as Junior Legion Baseball.

Still a "big kid", with his weight at around 219 pounds (about 100 pounds heavier than the average kid of that age) he played well, with a great batting average. He became well-known for his work ethic and for being a great teammate, as well as for hitting some impressively long shots.

During the summer coming up to his Senior year when he was 17, Tommy continued to excel at baseball, hitting a large number of home runs.

"Tommy, you are a liability to the team. You are slow. I am not going to cut you from the team, but I am also not going to play you either."

This was the message from Tommy's high school baseball coach the Spring of his Senior Year.

This was the coach's subliminal message. This was his code. And it worked perfectly. The message Tommy heard loud and clear was, "Tommy, you are still Too Big to Play. Go Home!"

And yet, Tommy was ready. He was resilient. And he was able to stand up for himself, even as someone he should have been able to rely on to truly care about him as both a player and a person let him down.

"Mom, Dad, I am going to go to every practice and every game. I am going to work hard and I am not going to quit. I will control what I can control and leave the rest up to God."

**Bullying victims are up to 9 times more likely to consider suicide than non-victims.**

Today, Tommy (now 23 and with his weight having peaked and now dipped to 193 pounds) has his own youth ministry where he leads and serves other children and young adults who are facing similar (or different) challenges.

Where he listens actively and with the intention to understand. Where he loves unconditionally. Where he connects authentically. And where he helps these people find the path that is right for them. Where he works to keep them safe.

**Research shows that victims of bullying are more likely to develop a psychiatric disorder, e.g., anxiety, depression, schizophrenia and substance abuse.**

But to get to this point has not been (is not) easy. And the mountain climbed is a true testament to Tommy.

Tommy too required mental health counselling to deal with the trauma from the bullying he suffered primarily at the hands of adults. To this day, every day, he continues to face the overwhelming darkness of anxiety head on.

Much like the sixty-year-old woman who recently shared, "Every time I have an opportunity to grow as a person. An opportunity to take a risk. An opportunity to move outside of myself... I still hear my 2nd Grade (ie aged 7-8) Physical Education Teacher telling me, 'You are not good enough'. So, I don't push past those boundaries and I miss grand opportunities to better myself. I am stuck."

Or the fifty-year-old man who learned early in life his worth (his value as a human being) was based solely on performance. On outcome. On achievement. He said recently, "I must be perfect. And if not, I am unworthy. I am nothing. When I was younger, I was told, 'If you do not win, don't bother coming home.' Those words still echo in my ears. ... I often think of suicide. Anytime I underachieve 'Don't bother coming home!' thunders and I want to die. I need more help."

Or the woman who confided that when she was in high school, her gym teacher would conduct the 'pinch test' to assess her level of body fat and then in front of everyone would call out the fat percentage and then add, "You are too fat. You need to be on a diet! And you will be running extra today!" To this day, this now thirty-four-year-old struggles with her self-esteem, with anorexia and with an addiction to exercise. "Every time I look in the mirror, what I see – I see through the lens of shame. 'I am too fat!' And I know I always will be."

Or the woman who when she was in primary school was told by her teacher that she was a 'pig' as the teacher flipped her desk over. And now nearly fifty years old this woman recently had bariatric surgery to prove once and for all to herself that she is not a 'pig'.

Tommy learned from his psychiatrist that he needed to talk to his own younger self... let's call him Young Tommy. To let Young Tommy know that he is and always has been loved. That what he experienced was wrong and not of his own doing. That there is no shame in being a victim of bullying (by anybody and especially by adults be they parents, coaches, teachers or others). That it is okay to be scared. And that Older Tommy is here now to help Young Tommy heal.

This is a daily conversation and not an easy one as the shadow and terror of anxiety often creeps back in. And yet, a conversation Tommy continues to have for and with himself and for all those children and young adults he is now helping.

## Fanning the Flame of Good

Back when Tommy was 8 years old, he wanted to play basketball.

Our hearts sunk. Will he be accepted? Will he be bullied? Will he get hurt physically, mentally, emotionally? How can we best support our boy?

With much fear on our hearts, we signed Tommy up for the local basketball program for eight-year-olds.

We would drop Tommy off at practice and on occasion watch the practice itself. But moreover, we would be at every game.

As we watched, I made note that most of the boys were quicker, faster, and more agile than Tommy and my boy did not appear to be having much fun. At this age, Tommy was around 100 pounds, when the average weight was around 80 pounds.

So, tapping into my quality and performance improvement background and leaning on my trust in God, I sought small and consistent win opportunities for my boy.

Physically Tommy was a big kid. And what can big kids excel at in basketball? That's right – rebounding. A rebound is when a player gains control of a basketball after a shot is missed. And to rebound really well one must learn to box out. Boxing out is a way for a player to position himself to best get a rebound after a shot has been missed. Sexy? No. Basic work? Perhaps. And yet, vital to a successful team at any level.

So, after viewing a few more practices and a couple of more games I realized that my boy (the "big kid") could be positioned to achieve some small and consistent wins.

And why was this important?

Was it important that Tommy's team win the championship? I don't believe at that age they kept count of the score, although I am sure the boys themselves did.

Was it important that I felt like a winner because my 8-year-old was a great ballplayer? I sure hope not.

The reason this was important was twofold: 1.) God gave Tommy a gift (a large frame), and 2.) Tommy deserved a win. With the bullying our son endured he deserved a chance to feel good about himself and especially and specifically because of who he truly is.

One day after school during the basketball season, Tommy and I went outside to the street where we have our own basketball hoop.

I showed Tommy how to get in position to box out, how he could "own" the semi-circle of space between him and the hoop, and the basic mechanics of boxing out. Together we saw how much easier it was to get the ball after a missed shot when we boxed out the correct way, with the right action, and I showed Tommy how his gift from God, his body, was so incredibly perfect for this important aspect of the game of basketball --- Fanning the Flame of Good.

The Friday evening before Tommy's next game (which happened to be at 8am on a Saturday morning) I could barely sleep. (Tommy slept soundly). I was so anxious. Was I doing the right thing? Did I put too much pressure on my son? Did I teach the box out correctly? But most importantly, was I doing the right thing for the right reason – again, right action for positive impact – and will Tommy have fun?

It is now shortly after 8am Saturday morning and Tommy takes his turn on the court. The quicker boys are flying up and down the court. They are laughing and joking and throwing up shot after shot and Tommy is struggling to keep up. My wife is cheering him on, and I am biting my tongue.

Soon Tommy is running near the sidelines and just loud enough so that only he can hear I say, "Tommy, remember your special gift from God --- box out."

Tommy looked up at me and I saw a very small but noticeable twinkle in his eye and that wonderful dimple that only appears when he smiles. "Box out," I whispered again.

Tommy's team is on offense. Tommy positions himself in the paint and I see him get in box-out position. He backs himself into one of the quicker and more aggressive boys on the other team and makes contact. He then remains attached to this boy like glue. Not necessarily a natural thing to do for a shy 8-year-old boy. Tommy's teammates dribble left. They dribble right. They dribble to the baseline and then back out to half court. And then a boy finally takes a shot.

Tommy is in good box-out position. The quick aggressive boy cannot get around him. The ball hits the rim, and then the backboard. And then... you guessed it... Tommy has boxed out well and gets the rebound. Now of course being a 39-year-old man at the time I respond with stoic resolve. Well, actually tears begin to flow freely down my cheeks as my boy, the "big kid", grabs his first rebound, pivots, and passes the ball to a teammate.

Tommy ends up with 8 rebounds for the game. But more importantly, after the game his dimple reappears as he shares with us how he boxed out and got rebounds and helped his team win.

Did his team win? I don't know. Again, I cannot even recall if the score was kept for the game. But there definitely was a win that day. Our son got his win. Perhaps in the big picture of life a small win. And yet to Tommy, and to my wife and I, a very big win. The "big kid" got his win.

The ride home we talked about how he boxed out and got rebounds. Walking into the house we talked about the number of rebounds. At lunch we relived the first rebound. The second rebound. The third rebound. We told Tommy how very proud of him we are. Not for the rebounds but for helping his team do well. And throughout these conversations I kept saying to God... "Thank YOU".

That afternoon Tommy asked me to play basketball with him again.

We went outside, and we did not discuss boxing out. Mostly we simply and quietly passed the ball to one another and took turns shooting.

Yes, Tommy got his *small* win. And then he built on it.

Throughout his first season, Tommy continued to combine the gift he received from God, with his knowledge of the game, his powerful desire to be of service to his team and continued to build upon each small win.

Each game his ability to anticipate when a shot would go up, where a rebound would come off the rim, and the direction an opposing player was likely to move to get the rebound improved to the point where he was being compared by coaches and parents alike to some of the top players in their youth.

And best of all, he smiled, and he laughed. For the first time in his life Tommy truly felt part of a team, of a community. His confidence grew. His self-esteem grew. And he had fun.

## A reputation

Tommy also developed a reputation, and no not a reputation due to the adverse impacts of being bullied, but another type.

Slowly at first, like the first ripple of a pebble penetrating a pristine crystal lake, and then greater and greater as the ripples became waves, we began to hear coaches (coaches of other teams) call out to their own players ...

> *"Boys! Rebound like number 15!"* or comment to those nearby *"Boxing out at 8-years-old?"* or huffing *"How many rebounds does that kid have?"* or (my personal favorite) *"I can't even get my High School basketball team to box out!"*

Yes, rebounds and boxing out. Coaches of competing teams, coaches of older teams, and of course Tommy's own coach all began to know Tommy as the eight-year-old boy who could AND would box out and rebound. The kid who did the important things to help his team. If they only knew the pain Tommy overcame each day and his resilience.

Riding home after Tommy's last game of the season the latest volley of feedback from coaches still rang in our ears:

> *"Wow ... I wish you played for me!" "I have never seen anyone attack the boards like you!"* and *"You are quite a ball player, I will be keeping an eye out for you."*

Quite the juxtaposition from "You are too big to play with other kids".

And as I looked in the rear-view mirror driving home that day, I could see Tommy smiling again from ear to ear as he relived his latest game, his past season, his win. Tommy's flame was burning.

## What a parent can do when a coach or teacher bullies a child

In any situation you come across where a coach or a teacher is in charge of young kids it is absolutely crucial to make note of how the coach is treating your child AND it is also critical to keep an eye out for how the other children are being treated as well. (In basketball lingo we call this "keeping your 'head on a swivel'", which means pay attention to what is in front of you but also to what else is happening around you.)

These are our communities and regardless of whom the child is, bullying behaviours are unacceptable, and it is incumbent upon us all to speak up for those who cannot do so for themselves and make a difference in their life. Bullying impacts at the acute time of bullying and often impacts over a long period of time.

---

Thomas and Tommy's story brings out some issues regarding the adult and child relationship between coach and child, as well as touching on how parents react to their own siblings sporting performances whilst spectating from the side lines.

I am left feeling that there is a question to be answered about what the purpose of facilitating children's sport is all about! Invariably there becomes a split of opinion, which often causes tension and unrest, no matter what the sport happens to be.

If the main aim is to develop and accommodate the skill and potential of a child, build up their confidence and provide them with equal opportunities to participate, then that's to be commended. As well as, of course, the huge health benefits of encouraging a love for regular physical exercise.

However, (and this is largely based on my own experience of watching my own children participate in team sport), I do feel that in many cases, whether coaches and parents like to admit it or not, the emphasis is on winning and on relying heavily on the **existing** skill level of a child, as opposed to their potential.

Often, as a parent we might see the potential of our child, but the coach has to make a call based on what they see, and their 'unbiased' decision is the one that counts!

When I watched my own son play junior football, I knew that the club focused all their teams on winning. Win, win, win was the sole aim. All through those years, even when the children were as young as 8 years old, it was rare to see visiting coaches, children and parents being content with losing the match.

If you have never watched a junior football game you would be amazed at the hostility and bad behaviour that often spills into the game, and this is just from some coaches and parents! Believe me, the children often swap places with the adults in the maturity stakes when the referee blows the whistle for the start of the game.

Let me just be clear here, such behaviour isn't a problem in every game, and it's usually just a minority of parents/coaches whose enthusiasm lets them down at times, but it isn't pretty when it happens!

I think that what Thomas did for his son Tommy is a great example to all parents. Rather than ranting and raving over what appeared to be a lost cause, he steadily and patiently coached his son. He did this because he knew, better than anyone, that Tommy had great potential which could bring a much-needed dynamic into the team. Thomas and Tommy working as their own little team unit became their only option, but one that paid off. Whether the coach or club should have nurtured his potential is the question, and one I am sure all parents in a similar situation would like answered for themselves.

Does bullying rear its ugly head in junior sport? Yes! I simply have no hesitation in answering that question in relation to football at least. It appears that once players cross the white line to play the game, some parents and coaches cross their own line of acceptable behaviour, and sadly I concur with what Bullying UK have posted on their website about this issue:

## Advice from Bullying UK for parents about bullying in sports

Bullying UK, part of Family Lives, receives complaints about what happens on and off the sports pitch too. It isn't just other players who can cause problems, but sometimes parents, coaches and team managers can also be capable of bullying behaviour.

## Pressure from mums and dads

Research shows that many youngsters give up football because of the stress of parental pressure, the shouting and taunts from the touchline. Football development officers often feel fed up with parents' behaviour, with mini soccer being turned into a mega stress with a 'win at all costs' attitude.

If parents are taking the game more seriously than they should, shouting vociferous encouragement from the side, displaying excessive disappointment at the missed goal and of course abuse or invasion of the pitch, this should not be tolerated and neither should abuse between rival team parents in the heat of the game.

## Set a good example

If you're a parent, think about the example you're setting to your child and other families. A friend of Bullying UK who managed a youth soccer team in Leeds told of one match where there was so much trouble that the police had to be called and they refused to let parents leave until they'd taken their car registration numbers. On another occasion when he substituted a player, the substituted boy's father, who was a linesman, threw down his flag in a display of petulance and shouted to his son: "Come on Thomas, we're going home".

The sports-mad parent may be pushing their son or daughter very hard and making unreasonable demands. Parents need to know that they can be guilty of bullying too and that constructive criticism about the effort they put in is acceptable but personal negative comments are not and neither is punishment for an off day.

If your child is being bullied in his/her sports club then talk to the coach or manager about it and ask them to make other staff aware of the problem. Ask for the matter to be dealt with discretely. If the coach catches the bully in action, they can't accuse the victim of telling tales.

## If the problem continues

If the problem continues and the club doesn't seem sympathetic, ask if there is a complaints procedure and follow it. Clubs may have their own rules or guidance issued by the sport's governing body and there may be appeal procedures over disciplinary matters.

If your complaint is about the coach, you need to be fair and objective when making a complaint. Not every child will be picked for the team every week and it's better to approach the coach in a friendly way to discuss any issues of concern. If you can't resolve matters at club level, you could consider taking it to the sport's governing body.

## How your child might feel

Remember that sport should be about fun and enjoyment and just because your child might not be as capable as another on the sports field doesn't mean that they should be left out. Sadly we know that this can happen and it can be heart-breaking for parents to watch their child having to sit on the touchline for excessive amounts of time, especially when they have attended training every week and have shown commitment to their club when others who are played haven't. If this continues to be an issue and you can see that your child obviously isn't enjoying their activity anymore then you might have to think long and hard about whether they should continue.

No one wants to see their child upset or despondent and if getting to games is starting to feel more like a chore than a joy, then you definitely need to sit down with your child and have a chat about how you might find a way forward. Focus on the positives – perhaps there is another club they can take a look at where things might not be so competitive, or another sport that they could try. It's imperative that you emphasise that they have done nothing wrong and don't deserve to be treated in this way, so they don't blame themselves.

Of course, you have the option of speaking to the club manager about this but try to remain calm and think about any impact this could have on your child in the future. Try to find out how your child would feel about you having a word with the manager beforehand.

Thank you, Bullying UK, for permission to reproduce these guidelines, which are a sensible, measured response to situations which can sometimes get out of hand.

Competitive sport teaches children all sorts of valuable skills, but it is that word 'competitive' which is the problem. It can be a positive word, representing striving for excellence through hard work and determination. But the flipside can be highly destructive:

competitive at all costs becomes dog eat dog, win at any cost, even if that means trampling over everyone else to become the winner.

All part of life's learning and hard knocks you might say, but when, in a junior sport environment, that trampling is sanctioned and even encouraged by everyone involved, it's time to step back and get a sense of perspective about the stakes involved. Is winning a junior league football match really more important than avoiding an eight-year-old's humiliation and shame?

# Chapter 7

# Death by Silence: Asha Clearwater's story

Most writers, at the best of times, find it challenging to create clear visions in their readers' minds based on their words alone. Asha Clearwater isn't one of them, it is simply second nature to her. In fact, her love of writing has been a big factor all through most of her life and she's really good at it.

So, when the opportunity came up for me to have Asha on board, I have to confess I still harbour some regret in having pondered on it for a few days until making my final decision. Why? Pure and simple, Asha is married to Taz Thornton, who recommended Asha and whose story is also featured, in Chapter 4. Hands up! I had presumed (falsely) that their stories would be too entwined. But Taz reassured me: "We both have our own personal stories, each different, and hers isn't mine to tell." Taz didn't add in "or vice versa," but I got it!

The form of bullying Asha has written about I am sure will awaken us all to think about how our words or lack of them can easily pierce someone else's soul like a poison arrow.

In preparation for Asha submitting her story, we had a chat on the phone, and it became clear that Asha is still quite hurt about the part of her past she is about to share, or at least in talking about it. And undoubtedly her love for Taz and the people close to her has made a massive difference since, and helped to give her the strength to have opened up with such courage and conviction.

Part of Asha's magnetism are her free spirit and her vulnerability – I strongly felt these sides to her personality. These are such endearing qualities and ones that I warmed to. Asha is one of those people who doesn't realise how special she is, always something that resonates when you meet someone like that.

Having listened to part of her story I know she cares deeply what people close to her think, especially about her sexuality, and what's come from her experience has brought her extreme sadness and heartache.

Asha sent me her story and told me the experience of writing and reliving it had been difficult. It's been very brave of Asha to talk about this part of her life, and I'm sure it will resonate with many of you when you read her beautifully written story. Her talents as a writer are supported by an impressive writing CV.

Asha Clearwater is an NCTJ (National Council for the Training of Journalists) qualified journalist who's been a news reporter, features editor and arts editor, as well as editor of several national business magazines.

Today, through her business Turquoise Tiger, she coaches SMEs on the art of great storytelling to promote their products and services. Asha occasionally freelances as a writer for national magazines and is even behind some of the information boards you'll find strolling through Woodland Trust Forests.

# Here's Asha's story...

I've never seen myself as a victim of bullying. At least not until recently and only since I've felt able to open up more about my past, thanks to the incredible kindness and compassion shown to me by a very close circle of friends. Writing this has been very challenging.

But now I'm going to put two words out there – Homophobic Bullying. Even typing these words brings that familiar lump to my throat and tears to my eyes. Perhaps you can feel it too. It's a horrible place to be and no-one deserves to be there, whatever their sexuality. In my view, where there's love there's God. Always. There's never a caveat: "Unless you're LGBTQ+".

Let's put this homophobic bullying in context. It's called Death by Silence.

Imagine the scene...

It's Monday evening. The phone rings. It's a family member at the end of the line. They talk, you respond. They talk some more. They tell you about their weekend – the kids, their work, the plans for the next week.

There's an awkward pause.

There are no questions about your weekend, your family, your furry kids, your plans for the next week, if you're lucky there's a cursory mention of your work – a safe subject obviously.

If you're feeling brave, YOU might crack the odd joke (this is your comfort zone, you've always been the funny one) and then go a step further, mention your family, some detail of your weekend including your wife's name. It's at this point that the silence at the end of the phone is so deafening it hurts.

You feel a stone in your heart and those damn tears pricking at your eyes again. But you say nothing. Instead you do the full Brit stiff upper lip thing, thank them for the call, say goodbye.

You hang up.

You repeat this little dance of sorrow time after time after time. Each time hoping with all your heart that things will be different. That one day they will ask questions about YOUR family, your love, your life, eager and genuinely pleased to hear your answers.

I have spent most of my life being a People Pleaser. But bullied? I didn't want to even consider that reality for a long, long time. So, what if I have gone along with situations, with people, with ideas, with plans for my future even when things haven't felt quite right. Isn't that what everybody does? Isn't that just compromising, playing the game of life?

I could have spoken up. I could have said "No". But I didn't.

I haven't been beaten, I haven't been threatened with violence, I haven't been mocked that much (directly, at least). In all truth I feel a bit of an interloper in these pages. But then a few memories flood in and I remember all those occasions where an invisible fist punched me right in the gut. I might not have been physically assaulted, but Death by Silence has certainly dealt me a thousand cuts. Sometimes, it wasn't so much the silence, as the barbed comments, or the weighted air between the words, that caused the damage.

If I think back, some of the first memories that come back, stinging as they hit my heart, are as follows:

- I was told by a close relative that my relationship with my female partner (now wife) had destroyed my parents. This comment haunted me for years – particularly as it was in stark contrast to my parents' actual reactions. They never, ever showed any signs of this with me, just demonstrated the very purest of love, and unwavering support, to both myself and my partner.
- When the relationship with my partner of several years was described, by a previously close family member, in dismissive terms, as 'this little arrangement'. I felt hurt beyond words and ashamed for me, my partner and my relative. I said nothing.
- When my partner and I were asked by other relatives to invent boyfriends for the evening while sitting in the car outside a family party. I laughed and, for the first time, in a long time, said "No". It felt good.
- When, not so long ago, we were told that we'd been put on a back table at a family wedding because no-one wanted to "sit with the lesbians". I was hurt, I was angry and I cried a lot. I love my family. Why could they not just love and accept me and my beautiful family too, even if it looked a little different to theirs?
- When a churchgoer, who had not seen me since the split with my husband, told me that she had been through a phase when she thought she had feelings for a female friend but had got through it. No acid tongue, no harsh words but plenty of thinly cloaked meaning and feeling and, I dare say, a prayer or two for me in the mix too. No matter that I hadn't asked for this. She (and God) knew best obviously... I was shocked and upset by her reaction, but said nothing, afraid of causing a scene. The me now would undoubtedly act differently.

Crossing boundaries without permission – a classic sign of bullying.

And these are just a few of the memories. Shared with no bitterness, no anger or regret, just a genuine wish that my words shared here may help another going through a similar kind of experience and support them to find the courage to make positive changes as I have now.

It's important for me to point out that this is not a religion bash. My parents, both Christian and now dead, loved my partner and I unconditionally. I have, no doubt, that my coming out, at the age of 30, must have been incredibly challenging for them, but they never allowed that to affect our relationship. We still went over for Sunday lunch, shared Christmases and New Year together, popped over for tea, laughed at the same silly things, shared stories of yesterday, today and tomorrow.

My parents loved us both and were always there for us. As it should be. I have met many, many Christians, and people from other faiths, who have had a truly positive impact on my life, and for who I am truly grateful.

However, when, aged 30, I fell in love with a woman I was, at regular intervals, brought face-to-face with the not so pretty side of 'Christianity' – the homophobic ignorance and bullying side that sometimes lurks behind closed doors. These people are not true Christians in my book. When is it right to prefer someone, like me, to stay in a marriage that was clearly not working – only making my husband and I miserable – rather than supporting me in becoming the person I was born to be.

Bullies exist in all walks of life and all situations, including some Church communities. They may not be on display IN the church – sometimes their true feelings only emerge outside of the pews and the pulpits and in more informal situations and relaxed company – but they DO exist.

How do I know this? Because I was privy to some of those conversations behind closed doors.

How we deal – or don't deal – with the experiences that challenge us, can have an immeasurable impact on our mental and physical health. I understand that now.

When I was going through those tough times, I just didn't deal with them very well at all. In true family tradition, I swept the not-so-good experiences under the carpet and left them to fester, like rotting fish in a heatwave.

I spent so many years trying to change – battling my own demons and trying to fight being attracted to women. At times, in the early days, I hoped and prayed my same sex attractions would go away.

Imagine all these feelings mixed with my people pleaser 'gene'. That heady mix was always destined to set me on the road to conflict, it's just that I never saw it until it was too late.

Through my turbulent teenage years, I allowed the People Pleaser in me to take over: I forged friendships where I had no voice and tried desperately to keep my friends happy at all times. We'd be on a night out and my answer to the question: "What would you like to do?" would invariably be the same: "I don't mind, what would *you* like to do?" or "I'm easy, whatever you want to do".

I would always be the one to go with the flow or at, least, that's what I used to tell myself, even if my addiction to people pleasing would sometimes leave me feeling stressed, lonely, sad, frustrated and sometimes, more than a little p****d off.

To this day, I drive my partner mad with the same responses from time to time. I have been caught in this pattern for a huge part of my life, and even now, it can be a hard habit to break.

I hated the thought of people not liking me if I said "No" to something. I couldn't stand it so, instead, I just kept quiet.

Sometimes, when I don't really want to admit that I might have been the victim of homophobic bullying – or, at the very least, emotional manipulation and disapproval – I try to blame my situation on my own fallback position of being a People Pleaser. Even when people were very clearly unhappy with my same sex relationship, I'd continually put myself in the emotional line of fire, going back time after time, seeking approval. It was all my fault, then, wasn't it?

There I would be, desperately clinging to the hope that things would change, that the people I loved would finally acknowledge my partner and the love we shared. The love was pure. If that isn't God at work than I don't know what is, I said to myself, so why couldn't my family members see it?

I so wanted their love and approval, I would go into full People Pleaser mode. I would make myself available for events and tasks, even if it meant having to rearrange my calendar and ditching my own family arrangements – all while knowing, in my heart of hearts, I'd be throwing myself into the lion's den again.

I wanted to show them I cared, while hoping they would do the same for me. But it made no difference. On each occasion, I was just unpicking the scab so it never truly healed.

In some of the old tribal traditions, the wise ones talk about dog medicine. Dogs – man's best friend – are loyal, the epitome of unconditional love. I know. I share my life with three of them. All beautiful, loving, loyal companions. They obey, they will follow you to the ends of the earth, they will protect you, they will even lay down their life for you.

In those ancient, teachings, the shadow side of dog medicine also reminds us that dogs will sometimes be so led by their need to please, to be loyal, that often they will keep going back to the human, even if they do not return that love, that loyalty, even, indeed, if they hurt them. Dog medicine warns us of the perils of going back, taking more and more punishment, until one day the loyal hound will either bite back or be beaten to death.

Dog medicine was my teacher for many years.

During those years, I tried to be everything for everyone – my churchgoing blood family and my own family. I did my best to express love for some of my blood family members at any cost, even while they refused to acknowledge the love I had for my wife and the love we shared.

Without any healthy boundaries in place, I was in danger of being that beaten dog. The one that snaps or, one day, doesn't get up again.

The same patterns had been repeating themselves again and again. And that slow, dawning realisation that things were not going to change, however much I aimed to please, was crippling.

Was it my fault, then? I can look back now and see that creating stronger boundaries, standing firm for me, for my love, stepping into my power – they were all my responsibility. So yes, to an extent, some of what happened – at least, allowing it to go on for so long – was on me.

But the judgement, the lack of compassion and understanding from those who were supposed to be my safety net, my armour, the people who were supposed to stand by me through thick and thin – that's on them.

I'm pretty sure I could have walked in front of a bus to save a child and it would not have been enough. *I* would never be enough. Once I left my husband and fell in love with a woman, the unconditional love and support I thought I had by default fell away.

Acknowledging this painful truth was a turning point in my life. It broke me in two and, for some time, left me picking up the pieces. But it was also a point when I began to finally set in place some healthy boundaries to preserve and protect my wellbeing.

I stopped calling, I stopped saying "Yes" to things.

Eventually, I walked away.

It was hard at first. But I did it.

Bullying comes in many forms. I know that now. My mental and physical state has shown me that, in glorious technicolour, over the past 20 years. It's also shown me that emotional bullying is real and can be just as devastating as other forms.

When bullying of any kind hits, it takes bullies to deliver the killer punches and there is no shortage of bullies in this world.

That punch always leaves bruises that need time to heal – regardless of whether they are visible.

If you've been 'punched', please acknowledge it. Don't bury your pain, or pretend it hasn't happened, or keep falling into those 'dog medicine' patterns that taught me such crippling lessons. Please – get the help you need – the help you deserve – and move on.

Always look forward. You deserve the very best future, even when that future is not the future others had planned for you. If you take nothing else from this chapter, then please remember this.

Today I'm me. 100% me, warts and all. Chatty, slightly kooky, often grumpy, hot-headed, but compassionate me.

Whether we meet via the wonders of social media, at a business meeting, in my local village hall assisting at a drumming and meditation evening or in the supermarket aisles, these days you'll always get me, unfiltered, real me. Not a cardboard cut-out version designed by others. And this is a great place to be. It feels clean. It feels right. It feels true.

Choosing to walk away from situations and people who didn't serve me, putting healthy boundaries in place, has been the best thing for my mental and physical health. A real life-changer in the best way.

I've been to the depths, I've wallowed in the muck, but now, I'm climbing higher and finally feeling the air in my lungs.

Today I'm running my own business – Turquoise Tiger – which like all of us, is in the continual process of change.

I work with solopreneurs and small businesses as a content coach, helping to turn them into powerful storytellers for their brand. Storytelling is in our blood and helping others to connect with this concept and share their unique stories to build trust and rapport with customers lights me up from the inside out.

Bringing in healthy boundaries has also had an incredibly positive impact on my work with Tiger. No more chasing the pound signs. No more soulless PR, pitch after pitch.

Now, I work with who I choose to work with, creating an uplifting and inspirational space where my clients are encouraged to become their own content creators to build their business. There's nothing like witnessing that light in their eyes when they finally see the true value of who they are and what they bring to the world. It's beautiful and a privilege.

These days you'll also find me helping to run workshops and spiritual retreats, promoting the awesome work of my wife, Taz Thornton, and accompanying her on international and UK wide speaking gigs, usually with a camera and/or a phone in hand to capture my beautiful pink haired powerhouse in action.

In 2019 I fulfilled a personal ambition and made history when I was awarded the licence for the first TEDxPeterborough – in my home city.

Together with a handful of fellow volunteers, we helped put Peterborough on the map by bringing speakers from across the world and the local community together to, in full TED style, share #IdeasWorthSpreading

The event received fantastic reviews and as I write this, I have just been awarded the licence for TEDxPeterborough in 2020. Another personal goal smashed. More exciting times ahead!

Who knows if I would have achieved any, or all, of this if my life had gone in the direction others wanted for me all those years ago? If I'd listened to those quick to judge?

What might have happened if I'd bowed to social pressure and 'played it safe', stayed in a heterosexual marriage, never followed my heart and let my love for another human being blossom, even when they shared the same reproductive organs as me.

None of this matters and, yet, it does matter.

It *so* matters.

It matters because #LoveisLove (I have a tattoo on my wrist so each day, especially those challenging days, I am reminded of this).

It matters because I, we, YOU, deserve love, deserve happiness and true happiness only comes when you let go of the judgements and expectations of others and live life for YOU.

Be true to you.

This last statement reminds me of a beautiful gift I received from my form tutor at school.

She was a big influence on my life and her words have stayed with me to this day.

On the last day of term with emotions running high (not surprising given it was a class of 30 teenage girls!), she presented us all with individual presents. Mine was a handmade quilted mirror with the words: "Always live your life so you can look yourself in the eye". Simple words, but powerful in their simplicity.

Thirty-five years later and they're still with me. They've been there to support, to hold, to reassure me. They've helped me break away from relationships and situations, just as I did when I finally said "No" to those homophobic bullies.

So, please live YOUR life for you, not for someone else, never settle for a watered-down version to keep everyone happy at the expense of your own happiness.

Take heart, set those boundaries, say "No", be prepared to walk away but with no regret or bitterness, just an eagerness to write your own story, to walk your own path your way.

When you do, the whole world opens up for you.

It has for me.

---

Thank you, Asha for such an emotional insight into what many of us who have read your story will feel isn't spoken about enough.

Homophobia is certainly one of the cruellest and hurtful forms of bullying, and one which I had not previously heard direct testimony. This subject has opened up my own mind and has been a much-needed form of personal education, especially as I am embarking on my own training with the amazing charity BulliesOut.

It was through meeting with the founder of BulliesOut, Linda James MBE, that I thought there was more going on in what Asha shared than first met the eye. Linda explained that I would be surprised at how many forms of bullying exist, and what she and her charity have to deal with; she was deadly serious and spot on. I have found more than even I thought possible when I originally conceived the idea to write this book and you can find out more about BulliesOut in Chapter 10.

Asha is right when she talks about the "not so pretty side of Christianity". It does exist, and the effects of it play a significant part in her story.

I really don't want to get into anything that comes over as controversial in this book, especially when it comes to Christian beliefs, but Asha's story will undoubtedly prompt some of us to at least ponder on what the Bible says about same sex relationships. Some reading this won't care, but Asha comes from a family of Christians, and she cares.

I think this answer given by Jimmy Creech, a former United Methodist pastor of nearly 30 years has merit, after he was asked the following question:

"What is at the heart of the position that the Bible is clear on the subject "that homosexuality is forbidden by God?"

Leach answered:

"At the heart of the claim that the Bible is clear "that homosexuality is forbidden by God" is poor biblical scholarship and a cultural bias read into the Bible. The Bible says nothing about "homosexuality" as an innate dimension of personality. Sexual orientation was not understood in biblical times. There are references in the Bible to same-gender sexual behaviour, and all of them are undeniably negative. But what is condemned in these passages is the violence, idolatry and exploitation related to the behaviour, not the same-gender nature of the behaviour. There are references in the Bible to different-gender sexual behaviour that are just as condemning for the same reasons. But no one claims that the condemnation is because the behaviour was between a man and a woman."

So, after spending a sizeable amount of time researching some aspects of what is depicted in Asha's story, I felt there were three entwined strands, all of which can exist separately but can often combine together, as in this case. Let's look at all three...

## Homophobic bullying

Homophobic bullying is when people behave or speak in a way which makes someone feel bullied because of their actual or perceived sexuality. People may be a target of this type of bullying because of their appearance, behaviour, physical traits or because they have friends or family who are lesbian, gay, bisexual, transgender, or possibly just because they are seen as being different.

## Being shunned by family

In families, a family member may be shunned or ostracized by a single person—the angry spouse, parent or child who refuses to speak or engage with them—or they may be shunned by the entire family. This is something that happens to many gay children when they come out or can happen to a family member who leaves the family religion or political affiliation or marries the wrong person.

> **❝ My self-worth is not linked to ❞
> your cruel words and action.
> My self-esteem is not affected
> by your deliberate attempts
> to destroy my character.
> You have no power over me.
> You will not silence me.**
>
> Marina Cohen

## The silent treatment

The silent treatment is the refusal to engage in verbal communication with someone, often as a response to conflict in a relationship. Also referred to as giving the cold shoulder or stonewalling, its use is a passive-aggressive form of control and can, in many circumstances, be considered a form of emotional abuse.

Below I quote from the leading LGBTQ+ charity Stonewall. Their name is derived from the Stonewall riots against police brutality towards the gay community in Manhattan in the late '60s. The Stonewall Inn was merely where the riots happened to start, but what an apt name it has turned out to be, with stonewalling forming such a toxic element of homophobic bullying.

In Asha's story, I felt there was more of an avoidance of acknowledging or even accepting her sexuality by some of her family, rather than an attempt at all-out stonewalling her. However, it appeared that it was the things not said or faced up to that really hurt Asha. In an ideal world, families should share through thick and thin and stick together, right?

I think we have those three layers working potently together here, mixed in, at least in this instance, with religious undertones, but all are most definitely under the umbrella of homophobic bullying.

The information I find common throughout my searches regarding homophobic bullying is that the written advice is aimed more at school children and teenagers than at adults.

# How common is homophobic bullying?

Homophobic bullying is the most frequent form of bullying after name-calling. According to Stonewall's School Report, 96% of gay pupils hear homophobic remarks such as "poof" or "lezza" used in school. 99% hear phrases such as, "That's so gay" or "You're so gay" in school. 54% of lesbian, gay and bisexual young people don't feel there is an adult at school who they can talk to about being gay. Worryingly, 6% of lesbian, gay and bisexual pupils are subjected to death threats.

I have a confession; I have spent hours looking for helpful information regarding how those who experience homophobic bullying might find help, but I don't feel that most of it is particularly different from general advice about bullying.

What seems to be evident is that looking or acting differently to "the masses" often poses a threat. If a man acts anything other than how a man "should" act, masculine, then they become a target. The same for women who don't demonstrate ultra-femininity, it's crazy! What seems particularly depressing is that right now, younger generations seem in so many ways more enlightened, more aware and more tolerant about many aspects of relationships and sexuality. There are now so many LGBTQ+ role models in sport, music and all parts of popular culture. So why do these pathetic taunts still happen?

I asked Asha what advice she might give to anyone starting to go through what she has gone through, so I will leave you with her words...

"Never apologise for being you. You are a beautiful human being free to love and be loved in a way that feels right for you. Never allow others to dictate how you should live your life. This is YOUR life and nobody else's so live it with a joyful heart."

Bullied Back to Life

# Chapter 8

# Sarah And Kay's story

This is the moving and emotional story of a mother & daughter on the very brink of tragedy, whose lives were almost certainly saved through sheer desperation when all appeared to be lost.

Sarah, 36 and her daughter Kay, 12, who live in Ohio, USA, are the closest a parent and child could be, and have relied on the strength of each other in the most difficult of circumstances most of us couldn't begin to comprehend. Both have had to deal with the cruellest of physical and mental bullying, both have suffered anxiety and depression, and both have been close to ending their lives because of suicidal thoughts.

I had to contact Sarah after she had posted something via social media about her daughter Kay's situation in being bullied at school, including a moving and heartfelt song Kay had written herself to bring some attention to her own plight in trying to deal with her situation... and it melted my heart!

Sarah is one of the most courageous and positive people I have ever had the privilege to speak to, yet she also demonstrates a significant level of vulnerability and deep emotion. All that is completely understandable considering what she has had to deal with throughout her life.

Sarah had posted stuff on anti-bullying websites and after I told her about me wanting to publish Kay's song in my book, there was extreme excitement in Sarah's voice, as she teasingly answered, "Of course but I will have to seek the song writer's approval first!"

After getting the OK to include Kay's song I asked Sarah to share some of her and Kay's story and after hearing what they have been through, and are still going through, I asked if I might also include some of it in this book, as I felt it would touch the hearts of many more people in similar situations.

Sarah clearly expressed her desire to stand up to bullying and talked it through with Kay, and soon agreed subject to their joint approval of what we write from our interviewing sessions. We agreed to go to our first draft, but I was aware that we needed to be sensitive in our approach.

I spoke and communicated with Sarah several times before I felt she fully trusted me to help tell her and Kay's story, and I felt so privileged. Before sharing their story, what would be more fitting than starting with Kay's song?

*Oh, oh we are all the same you can't blame me, this is not a game*

*Now listen to me, we are all human, this is just time-consumin', boring as watching paint dry*

*We don't want to live this way x 3*

*Bullying is not OK x 2*

*They get us in the blind spot, it's like a never-ending bad dream, it's a day you will never forget yeah-a-yeah in the blink of an eye, time goes past*

*It's a hot potato, it's a huge issue, that keeps on going and going and never stops but gets worse*

*It's like a curse from Mr. Universe*

*It's everywhere, it's in the air x 2*

*People think it's rare, it's more common than you think, sadly people just ignore it*

*Bullying is not OK x 2*

*We don't want to live this way x 4*

*It feels like school's a death trap*

*It's just cruel, you're left with a broken heart, bullying is like a creature of the school, it feels like a stabbing pain*

*This needs to be stopped, we're all human, we are all different in our own way, it's kinda like a never-ending Monday*

*Yeah, it's a curse from Mr. Universe*

*It's a blinding light x2*

*Ohhhhhh yeah yeah yeah x2*

# Sarah & Kay's story (told by Sarah)

Difficulties started when Kay was diagnosed with epilepsy during kindergarten at the age of only six. Various attempts at medication followed, and then the early stages of depression started to manifest themselves. ADHD was given as the reason for a change in Kay's behaviour patterns and I then noticed the reactions of others who came into contact with her also change. The bullying started with a few pushes at first, before becoming cruel mocking and alienation from her peers later during school. It was clear they couldn't comprehend a young girl looking and acting "differently," someone who was struggling to fit in.

Over the first few tentative years of schooling, Kay began to get behind in her schoolwork, as depression took hold and she was soon experiencing feelings of suicide.

And then, to compound the situation even more, I suffered a life-threatening head injury that led to a series of seizures, and the recovery process was very slow. This was too much for me to cope with and I spiralled into anxiety and deep depression myself. Prescribing the right medication was far from straightforward and my situation was bleak!

Looking back now, I find it hard to know how I got to that point, as the drugs did little more than confuse me. It was like a fog had descended in my head, life was a blur and I was literally hanging on.

My focus and concentration levels were significantly affected, and it was becoming a real issue.

Somehow, I managed to muster the strength and raise myself out of the darkness and into a light shining so bright that I didn't see it coming. No, I am not talking about religion, although I do have my own personal spiritual faith. I was fighting for Kay; she needed me, and I had to muster every ounce of strength in my inner being, despite feeling there was very little left.

You see, when the medical profession couldn't or wouldn't find the answer in 18 months of trying, the outcome seemed hopeless until a last-ditch Google search culminated in new hope and renewed life. I wanted to find a distraction, maybe a hobby or something that might give me purpose, and I received much more than I ever thought possible.

The life saver was art, canvas painting and sketching to be more precise, and it would begin to heal the damage, ease the pain and become a therapeutic remedy no one could have seen coming. The Google search brought an unlikely answer that I strongly feel any prescribed drugs or medicine would have failed to bring.

I remember literally hunting through my house for some paint and a few brushes, and it wasn't long before I started to feel the effects of healing through my painting. My days turned from the dismal grey to reflect the bright colours I began to paint on the canvas and I wasn't half bad at it either!

A huge comfort for me is to know that the sharing of our story will help inspire others who suffer any form of oppression. I found a way to self-heal and impress my wisdom and guidance into Kay's life in a way I couldn't have contemplated, and it culminated in joy as Kay took to the canvas herself. Although our problems are still ongoing, our art sessions have brought us even closer together and it makes our pain more bearable!

We discuss what is happening at school and Kay opens up. I try to encourage her to keep being the wonderfully talented person she is, and it's amazing how she gives such incredible strength back to me.

Kay has endured cruel jibes and school-ground bullying for over half of her life due to being "different" to the rest of her class. She has already had to deal with much more than most adults have to put up with in a lifetime, and I am always telling her that is a real good thing. Not many people get to experience the emotions and upheaval Kay has endured and to me that puts her ahead of the crowd and that makes us proud; it's like a maturity and appreciation of what life can really be like, and we've had a lot come our way.

Being different should be embraced and celebrated, but unfortunately, we don't live in that kind of world. Still, we always live in hope that this will change. I try so desperately hard to keep Kay upbeat and free from anger or resentment, and one small step at a time, we are getting there.

It's slow working progress and a daily battle, but there is brilliant light included in the darkness of the day when we get together to paint and sketch. By doing that we have discovered that we can express our feelings in our art and find an escape.

---

**Thank you, Sarah for sharing this story.**

*"If your daughter was more normal none of the bullying would have happened."*

It has become clear to me that Sarah doesn't want to cast a dark shadow over what has happened and continues to happen. Yes, she feels let down, like her cries for help have fallen on deaf ears, in a system designed to function without allowance for any "rocking of the proverbial boat," or provision for special needs.

Make no mistake though, there wasn't a hint of bitterness or contempt in Sarah's voice as she described some of the stuff she and Kay have gone through together. For instance, Sarah was told by an "authority figure" at Kay's school, whose identity she wants to keep to herself, that "If your daughter was more normal none of the bullying would have happened."

Can you imagine? Undoubtedly Sarah was hurt, really hurt, but several months later, in talking about it to me about that "dagger in the heart statement," she found a moment to make light of the situation. "If they think Kay is weird, they don't yet know how weird I can be", she said before chuckling. And I totally got what she meant. These two come as a team, mother and daughter; if one is hurt the other feels the pain and if one is labelled, the other shares the label, that is until the time comes when the world begins to understand and take action.

> **66 When you hold people up 99 for ridicule, you have to take responsibility when other people act on it.**
>
> — Hannah Baker

Sarah then shared these further thoughts:

"Kay has been pushed and is frequently the butt of the jokes of the children in her class, so it gets cruel and messy sometimes. When you stoke the fire, the flames can burn fiercely and Kay has reacted; she finds it hard not to, who wouldn't? She doesn't know how to control her feelings sometimes and is confused and sad and is often the one blamed for flare-ups. I think it's easier for teachers to point towards Kay as the problem rather than sorting out the wider, deeper issues that these children have with one person.

"I have learned, and also teach Kay, that success is not measured by our bank accounts, the jobs we have, even by the quality of our health, because all that can be taken in a heartbeat. We have had it happen... multiple times. **We measure success by our hearts, the way we treat people, and the kindness we do for others. Those are the things that matter in the end. None of the rest of it really does.**"

Now, those are sentiments we can all use to help us to get through tough times and face the future.

Sarah understandably found sharing too much detail difficult, as she stated the following, "Long after this book is out there for the people to read, Kay and I have to carry on our fight to gain acceptance in our community, so we could do without the extra attention." I assured Sarah that part of the criteria of my book is not to name names or pass on shame, and I knew she wanted to be part of this as much as anyone; I was so proud of her and Kay!

I told her that I want this book to become one small part of the catalyst for the beginning of change in our society, in schools, in the workplace, in the cyber world and in homes. I promised Sarah that her contribution, along with all the others whose personal accounts are also included, would help change lives. I couldn't promise her how many people would read my book, or that it would actually make the impact to the kind of level I want, in the same way she couldn't be certain of changing her and Kay's destiny to the level she wants. But I could promise her hope. **We all have hope!**

Sarah made it clear she didn't want to focus on herself and her own experiences of bullying as a child; her main concern was Kay. She also didn't want to go too deep into some of the incidents that have occurred during Kay's schooling; she doesn't see any purpose in taking them all up or pointing the finger.

Yes, there is a feeling that Sarah's voice falls on deaf ears and that the support she and Kay so desperately need isn't there, but she is doing all she can to learn about what other channels of advice and support might be available. Having self-educated in this way she has already managed to secure some great one-to-one counselling for both her and Kay.

The one thing that has touched me the most in what Sarah has shared with me is the way she encourages and teaches Kay to demonstrate kindness to her mockers and tormentors at school, despite the sadness and loneliness she feels. I wouldn't have blamed Sarah for harbouring bitterness and animosity, but she displays no trace of resentment toward the arbitrators and the administrators of their pain, past and present. Yes, the sadness is there in her voice; her emotions flip from her almost crying to being joyful, sometimes in the same sentence. But Sarah has an amazing sense of humour and often laughs at the absurdity of how life unfolds. Maybe that's how she copes. I have known that feeling too but it doesn't mean the hurt isn't ever present.

I have loved bringing this unique and inspirational story into these pages. I was so wowed by the richness of talent Sarah possesses; you only have to see the wonderful life she has brought to the canvas. All her work tells a story and reflects how she is feeling at that particular moment and then her talent just takes over. And I know without doubt that Sarah, regardless of whether her art was of such a high quality level or not and she wouldn't have minded either way; it's how it all helped transform, or dare I say, helped save two lives that is really important!

Sarah is an intelligent and warm person who has had to take the knocks that came and still continue to come her and Kay's way. She is also a strong lady (she has simply had to be to survive) and this has also stood out to me as I have heard how she has used this asset to stand up against so much adversity.

Just go to this link to see Sarah's website that displays some of her amazing art collection, and maybe, if you look deep enough, you might just learn more about this truly gifted and inspirational individual. Go to:

https://fineartamerica.com/profiles/1-sarah-neumann/shop

And finally...

There are resources throughout areas of my book that advise on how children and parents can deal with bullying in school. For that reason, I wanted to dedicate the closing part of this chapter to displaying a small selection of Sarah's pictures.

I hope you have found this story as inspiring as I did!

Bullied Back to Life

# Chapter 9

# UK research and resources on bullying

Right now, so many areas which affect our wellbeing and our mental health are being explored, investigated and scrutinised in a way never seen before. This is of course a welcome trend and one that points the way to a more open, confessional, accepting and healing way forward on all sorts of fronts.

Current abuse, historical abuse, intolerance of race, religion or orientation are all being called out. Past generations and previously established attitudes seemed to accept a "sweep it under the carpet" approach – don't rock the boat, don't cause trouble, don't rake up pain from the past.

This new spotlight is forcing into the open much that has been left unspoken, smashing the British habit of not speaking out, recognising that nothing should be off-limits when it comes to squaring up to forces which have caused pain and suffering over decades and even over generations.

Many of these issues relate to bullying of one sort or another: child abuse, sexual abuse, domestic violence, fat-shaming… the list keeps growing. It is not within the scope and purpose of this book to look at every manifestation of bullying. Our focus is on childhood and workplace bullying, but this opening of the floodgates and fresh climate of openness is leading to a growing body of evidence which can be used to underline the stories told in this book.

Bullying surveys, anti-bullying events and 'weeks', charities, alliances and self-help organisations focused on combatting bullying are springing up and growing all the time. These are all helping to give voice to this emerging #MeToo spirit. Hopefully, this book won't be seen as bandwagon-jumping on the back of this movement, as my motivation to write this goes back many years on the back of my experiences from decades ago; it is just timely that it coincides with this new confessional era. I have trawled the web for all sorts of background information for this book and, as with any topic, the amount of information online can be bewildering.

I have picked out some of this material for comment. I have focused solely on UK-based information, as this feels more relatable than US-based material. Not surprisingly, the vast majority of online resources and research findings are aimed at the sector of bullying activities towards young people and below are comments based around a couple of the most prominent sites. As I am also interested in the effects of bullying on adults, I have extended my search there as well, and again, there is some information about that issue in this chapter.

**So, what is this wave of bullying research and awareness telling us?**

I guess what I'm learning from many of these sources will not come as a surprise: bullying is everywhere and is affecting most of us. That "most" is not an exaggeration. For example, the most recent annual bullying survey by one of the most authoritative groups in the UK, Ditch the Label (www.ditchthelabel.org) concludes that 51% of 12-20 year olds surveyed had experienced some form of bullying in the past year.

This pervasiveness is being fuelled by the no-hiding-place tyranny of bullying via social media and smartphone. Again, it is not my intention to focus greatly on cyber-bullying, as this is a relatively recent phenomenon and not one where I can bring any personal experience to bear.

However, the root causes, motivations and effects of cyber-bullying are really not so very different from the old-fashioned in-the-room playground/workplace bullying that I talk about elsewhere in this book. Mindless discrimination against anyone who is 'different' in any way; the power kick the bully seems to enjoy; the relentless pursuit of a person way beyond the root cause of the bullying, however trivial that may have been; the scent of blood by the baying herd of followers; the lack of awareness of the sharpness of the pain caused – these have always been there and are now just able to be enacted at the touch of a screen and shared instantly, 24/7. This of course puts bullying literally into the hands of everyone holding a phone. Without even leaving their chair, someone can inflict pain and humiliation on a constant basis, and there are many who seem to be doing just that.

But this growth in bullying is being met with a (hopefully) equal and opposite force of those prepared to stand up, name it and call it out. So, let's find out more about the current research and activity on bullying in the UK.

I would strongly recommend that you take a look at Ditch the Label, which refers to its website www.ditchthelabel.org as "the largest anti-bullying support hub in the world." Its focus is on those in the 12-25 age group and it works closely with schools, colleges and online communities to help to raise awareness of the extent of bullying, and to combat it. As my own formative experiences of bullying show, it is exposure at that vulnerable age that can mark you for life. That is what makes their work so important.

# Bullying survey

Ditch the Label conducts an Annual UK Bullying Survey and the 2018 survey is the sixth they have conducted, gathering close to 10,000 detailed responses from young people right across the UK. The survey report is available as a downloadable pdf from the Ditch the Label site. Interestingly, it gives almost equal scrutiny to three types of people: victims of bullying, perpetrators and (new in 2018) witnesses. Reading about these three different perspectives is fascinating, as what becomes clear is that all three types are in fact victims. A sizeable percentage of bullies feel guilty or upset about their actions, although a fair number do also feel excited or powerful as a result of their actions.

With the witnesses, only a tiny percentage thought the bullying they saw or were aware of was funny or enjoyable. The vast majority felt bad, upset or guilty, or felt threatened that it could also happen to them. The majority of witnesses did claim to perform some sort of intervention on behalf of victims, but again this led to feelings of powerlessness and fear.

This triangle of bully, victim and witness is a fascinating one to consider, particularly as often a key motivation for the bully is to perform in front of an audience, to exert power and influence not only on the immediate victim, but to intimidate and even feel they are impressing a wide circle of people with their actions. It marks out their territory, creates their 'manor', their fiefdom, their domain. A single but powerful act of bullying on one person can be a calling card: step out of line and its your turn next; I now have power over this entire school group/workplace/social circle.

## Calling out the bullies

However, as commented on earlier in this chapter, reliance on that unquestioning acquiescence across a group is now becoming far more difficult. The climate is changing. People aren't just thinking enough is enough, they are saying it too, calling people out publicly. This of course often takes great courage and can carry considerable risk. You can take a stand and look behind you and find that no-one else has stood up alongside you. But I like to think that the chances of others rallying to your actions are increasing every day as the boundaries of what is acceptable behaviour are drawn ever more visibly and sharply.

## More information on bullying

An authoritative source of information is the Anti-Bullying Alliance (ABA), which is was established back in 2002 by the NSPCC and the National Children's Bureau (NCB). The NCB hosts their website, www.anti-bullyingalliance.org.uk. This site has a wealth of resources and is also aimed predominantly at young people.

A key programme within The Diana Award, founded as a legacy to Diana, Princess of Wales' belief in the power of young people to change the world, is its resources and awards built around its anti-bullying campaigning. You can find out more at www.antibullyingpro.com.

## Anti-Bullying Week

ABA are the official organisers of Anti-Bullying Week, which takes place in November each year. Each year there is a theme to the week, and in 2019 the theme was **'Change Starts With Us'**. Anti-Bullying Week creates an excellent framework for schools, parents and carers to focus on bullying and its effects.

The 2019 theme is one that resonates strongly with the stories in this book. A rallying cry across all the stories, including mine, has been just that: **'Change Starts With Us.'** Change starts with a conversation, with EVERYONE working together to call out bullying and to find ways to end it. However small each person's contribution is to the debate and to this huge challenge, cumulatively this is the only way to make a big difference. Policy makers and institutions such as churches, schools and local authorities can all do their best to create a 'top down' zero tolerance climate towards bullying. But none of that will gain real traction and have a grass roots effect within classrooms, families and workplaces if individuals everywhere aren't making a stand, breaking the taboo of silence and talking about it. Please get involved!

## BulliesOut

All proceeds from sales of Bullied Back to Life will be going to my chosen charity, BulliesOut. For more info visit bulliesout.com

In purchasing this book, you will have already helped towards changing and saving lives in the future. If you find that hard to believe, read on...

Bullied Back to Life

# Chapter 10

# BulliesOut

**E**very penny made through the sales of this book will go to **BulliesOut,** the wonderful charity I came to know about during my research and whose helpful information I have used throughout these chapters. I recently became a volunteer for BulliesOut myself and I am looking forward to doing what I can to help.

# About BulliesOut

BulliesOut, one of the UK's most important anti-bullying charities, provides help, support and information to individuals, schools, youth and community settings, and the workplace. Their award-winning work addresses one of the core issues affecting a person's emotional, social and academic well-being.

BulliesOut has grown from being a simple web-based advice service to a provider of comprehensive programmes of workshops and training. The charity works with the bullied, bully and bystander and engages, empowers and inspires people to #StandUpSpeakOut against bullying. Please use that hashtag to search for relevant comments online and use it yourself as a message to others.

I caught up with Linda James MBE, the founder of BulliesOut, over a cup of coffee or two in Cardiff in August 2019. She had two very important people with her: Emma, one of her key workers, who gives up so much free time to help move the charity forward; and her lovely aunt Rose, who was such a delight. Emma knew Linda before she set up the charity and has been with her from the start. She gave me some invaluable insight into the setting up and running of BulliesOut. Aunt Rose chipped in with her views on how bullying was simply an accepted behaviour in her younger life; I could tell that her support for Linda was highly appreciated and valued.

Becoming the catalyst for change is very often a thankless and lonely journey to embark on and it takes someone truly special to swim against such strong currents of resistance, especially over a long period of time. Linda James is one of those rare breeds of people.

As we chatted, I could immediately feel Linda's undeniable passion for what she and her charity stand for as she gave me a powerful overview before articulately painting her vision moving forward.

It was also very clear that Linda has no time or interest in warming herself in the glow of her achievements, the MBE included. They are not why she does all this work, but merely its by-product. Having said that, of course Linda is proud of receiving acknowledgement from the Queen, who wouldn't be?

As Linda opened up more, she spoke about many of the challenges in dedicating her life to her charity. I was so enthralled I couldn't keep up with my notes, so I have made sure she has double-checked what I have written. Here's Linda's testimony from that interview.

# Linda's story

"I was bullied between the ages of 11 and 16. It was an awful experience that left me lacking in confidence and self-esteem. I was never an outgoing child (due to challenging family circumstances) but found myself withdrawing even more. I developed an eating disorder at the age of 14, tried to take my own life twice (aged 14 and 17) and at 16 I left school without sitting my formal exams. As an A/B student who wanted to be a nurse (preferably in the Navy), this ended my career.

"When my son was bullied at the age of 10, it brought back the negative experiences that had happened to me and I decided I was not going to let that happen to him. Sadly, his school at the time wasn't very supportive and there wasn't any anti-bullying support locally so this (along with the comment of "Set up the help then Mum" from my son) inspired me to do something about it. I wanted to set up an organisation which could provide support to those who needed it."

I then asked Linda if bullying, in her experience, is still seen as taboo.

"I don't feel bullying is "taboo" anymore. There is far more awareness now. However, many schools have had their budgets cut and this impacts on their spending. Unfortunately, bullying is not a standalone compulsory subject on the curriculum – it falls under the collective PHSE (along with sexual health, healthy eating etc) so the budget allocated for this subject needs to go a long way.

"Some funders initially see our work as "education", which of course it isn't. Many of them won't fund "education" or work on it within a school environment, so this does make it difficult when applying for funds to deliver our sessions free of charge. The Welsh Government certainly recognise the issue, but they don't support us to do anything about it.

"We work hard for funding and we are doing OK – we have grown the charity over the years, but of course there is obviously room for more financial support."

BulliesOut do a lot of work in schools and in 2018 they successfully reached out to 7,000 children; I asked Linda what support there was in this charity/school collaboration.

"Bullying is an issue that removes confidence and self-esteem, and this is where the problem is for individuals. They don't report it as they feel embarrassed, scared and humiliated. Schools don't like to highlight it too much as they're worried parents won't send their children there and the school budget will be impacted even more. It's a vicious circle!"

Linda shared with me that the work BulliesOut has undertaken in only the last few months has saved two young people from committing suicide. This is the moving testimonial of one of those youngsters...

My name is Casey-Jane and I have been a Youth Ambassador with BulliesOut for 3 years.

Before I joined BulliesOut I was using the mentor service, as I was going through very bad bullying in school and outside of school.

I was bullied for 8 years (from the ages of 4 to 12) and the mentor service has provided me with two years of vital support, before telling me about the YA programme.

I applied for the YA programme in November 2015 and got accepted in early 2016. I was so nervous to attend my first meeting with BulliesOut, but everyone made it so easy! It was the best experience! At the time, meetings were bi-monthly (they're now monthly) and were based in Cardiff.

Joining BulliesOut has given me so much! I have gained so many skills including: mindfulness, resilience, acting, breathing strategies, peer2peer training and so much more!

Being a YA, I have also had the opportunity to gain a Youth Achievement Award. I took that opportunity and I achieved my bronze award. After that I had the opportunity to continue, so I then achieved my silver award.

I have also made so many lifelong bonds with people, Linda especially, as when I joined, I was going through a lot of trauma at home; domestic abuse/violence, drug abuse and substance misuse.

All of that was going on and I didn't trust anyone except Linda. She was the most supportive.

From being a YA I have met some people who have helped change my life. Because of my past, I suffer from anxiety and PTSD and in December, I hit a low spot and was considering suicide. BulliesOut held an awards event to recognise our achievements and I was recognised at this event. I also met some great people there who had also overcome personal challenges. One speaker changed my life completely. He shared his story and how he got through it and he chose me to share mine and afterwards he said God was telling him to pick me and from then on, I've let nothing stop me.

BulliesOut sent out an email in early 2018, to apply for the Welsh Youth Parliament. I was encouraged by BulliesOut to apply and so I did. I was put through to the general elections and I am now the Welsh Youth Parliament Member for the Cynon Valley. **Thanks to BulliesOut I am now who I want to be.**

Becoming a YA was the best thing I've ever done. I wanted to join BulliesOut because I know what bullying can do to someone and I didn't want anyone to have to go through that. Having a BulliesOut jacket to wear all the time helped in my community because people felt safe talking to me and that is a feeling I cannot explain.

Being a YA made me stronger, more confident and gave me a purpose when I needed one the most. Being a YA has honestly changed my life.

If you're reading this and need, or know someone who needs, a purpose or wants to make a difference, join BulliesOut. It's honestly the best thing I have ever done.

---

Thank you, Casey-Jane, for sharing that honest and inspiring story.

Emma, who volunteers for BulliesOut, told me that talking about bullying is like how we used to deal with cancer a few decades ago. It is whispered about behind closed doors and not faced up to.

We are now living in a more advanced world and yet people are still committing suicide. We all should share the responsibility, and as Ray Dawson said in his story, make it our business! That 2019 Anti-Bullying Week theme comes to mind again: **Change Starts With Us**.

At the beginning of this book I said, "I didn't think I was even worth the apple someone threw in my face." Sounds a little dramatic doesn't it? But that's exactly how I felt! I hated the attention I was getting and, at times, wanted the playground to open up and swallow me whole. But somewhere inside me there was a flicker of a small flame. That flame nearly went out; one more beating and it might have happened, but I consider myself fortunate that now that flame has turned into a burning furnace in my being.

I know that so many people have experienced and endured much worse than me and many continue to do so. Some have got through and some haven't. This book is a tribute to all those who have battled and made it through. More than that though, it is also designed to be an inspiration to those who are facing the struggle right now. Take strength from the stories here, **proof that anyone can be Bullied Back to Life.**

As with many anti-bullying organisations, BulliesOut primary focus is on young people, but they also have a comprehensive programme which helps to tackle workplace bullying too, with training courses for employers and employees. On their website they quote a recent survey sponsored by the TUC, that **1 in 3 employees** felt they had been bullied at work and 30% have witnessed bullying in the workplace. BulliesOut run courses and provide training material to raise awareness among employers of the scale of this issue and offer ways in which this can be overcome.

Another staggering statistic which BulliesOut quote is that bullying currently causes the loss of 18 million working days every year. So, bullying is directly affecting the productivity of the nation's workforce and in this way is denting the profitability of companies right across the UK.

My primary concern is the effect that bullying has on the mental and physical wellbeing of all the people affected, but by also relating it directly to the profit and loss of the UK's businesses, there is a stronger chance that companies will take the issue seriously and dedicate HR resources to eradicate it within their organisations. Absenteeism as a result of bullying is likely to be given every reason other than bullying by the person who goes off sick, which of course makes it harder to spot and more difficult to put right. This is where employers need to be close to their workforce, picking up on the tell-tale warning signs within the workplace of intimidation, cliques, petty point-scoring, intolerance of the 'different'. There are many types of workplace bullying, many of which can be subtle. But subtle may still be deadly; insidious, creeping and menacing, in many ways this may be harder to live with than a pointless nudge in the canteen.

BulliesOut have a highly effective slogan which they link to this '18m+ days' statistic: **Break The Silence. If You Don't, Who Will?**

It's up to every employer and every employee to call out workplace bullying, before one of their colleagues, usually a fit and healthy person, suddenly starts taking unexplained periods of time off work and stops being an enthusiastic and outgoing member of staff. Employers have a legal duty to protect their staff and protecting people against bullying falls within that legal duty.

## Adult bullying

Elsewhere in this book, we have shown the effects of bullying in adult life, and just how devastating and long-lasting its effects can be. It is therefore vital that resources are available for adults as well as for children and schools. So, it is encouraging to see that there are some organisations in the UK which adults can turn to.

The National Bullying Helpline, www.nationalbullyinghelpline. co.uk, is a voluntary run helpline and a nationally recognised advice centre on all aspects of bullying. On their site is a large section dedicated to advice and support on all aspects of workplace bullying, with resources for employers and well as for those who are victims.

The **National Bullying Helpline** number is 0845 22 55 787 and it is available Monday to Friday, 9am to 5pm.

ACAS (The Advisory, Conciliation and Arbitration Service) provides free and impartial advice to employers and employees on all aspects of workplace bullying and harassment. Indeed, the Government itself provides advice on these issues, and these can be found on the gov.uk site.

## Helplines and charities

A Google search on bullying quickly reveals a large number of national and local helplines, charities and other voluntary and advisory organisations all offering help and support to victims of bullying. I'll leave you to conduct your own online research.

A helpline can be a vital lifeline for anyone who is at the end of their tether and has no-one else to turn to. As well as the National Bullying Helpline there are a number of other helplines, all operated by trained professionals, who can help. Here are some others which may be of relevance:

- **ChildLine:** The UK's free, confidential helpline for children and young people, offering advice and support, by phone and online, 24 hours a day. Probably the UK's most well-known helpline, offering invaluable support for decades now. **Call 0800 1111.**

- **EACH:** A freephone helpline for children experiencing homophobic, biphobic or transphobic bullying or harassment: **0808 1000 143.** It's open Monday to Friday 10am-5pm.

- **BullyBusters:** Based on Merseyside, BullyBusters started out as a confidential freephone helpline back in 2004 and has now expanded to provide a whole range of anti-bullying services. For more information visit www.bullybusters.org. uk. The BullyBusters helpline is **0800 169 6928**.

These are just some of the more prominent anti-bullying helplines which come up in a Google search for 'Bullying helplines'; if you are looking for a helpline, best to conduct your own online search, particularly for helplines and organisations local to you.

## What about the over 25s?

If you are over 25 it's easy to feel somewhat disenfranchised, as most support is (understandably) aimed at children and young adults. This is of course the most at-risk group, with the school environment and high social media usage the ideal hothouse environment for bullies to grow and thrive.

My trawl through the web does underline my feeling though that this spotlight on under 25s is inevitably diverting resources and attention away from the insidious life-long effects that bullying can have well into middle- and old-age.

Certainly, my own experience is one of bullying that took place when I was under 25 continuing to affect my life for many years beyond that period. This book is my attempt to come to terms with that and share that feeling with others who may also be experiencing these significant after-shocks from events which occurred decades ago. I suspect there are tens of thousands of over 25s (and over 50s!) who are still grappling with the legacy of bullying which occurred earlier in their life. If you count yourself among them, then this book is most definitely aimed at you.

Bullied Back to Life

# Chapter 11

# Be Bullied Back to Life

**M**y aim has been to write a book about a cross-section of people who have gone on to find success despite being badly beaten, ridiculed, humiliated and in some cases, almost bullied to death.

As you will have read, success, in the context of this book, *Bullied Back to Life*, has nothing to do with monetary or professional gain, but everything to do with winning back self-confidence and being released from the clutches of our bullies.

Simply put, those of us whose stories you have read in previous chapters: **we are standing up together and making a statement that enough is enough. I hope we have inspired those of you who are going through or have been through this dreadful and demeaning act of intimidation to one day feel strong enough to stand with us.**

To those of you who have been lucky enough to not feel the weight of how bullying can negatively affect your life, this book might have been more about getting on with fulfilling some of your own potential without seeking permission from anyone who hasn't your best interests at heart, past or present; I hope at the very least, it has done that for you!

I have felt humbled and proud having written this book, despite certain people's advice to "perhaps consider changing the subject matter." And if any of you who offered that advice are reading this now, I know you only meant well, but as much as I love you, I never had any intention of taking it.

**You weren't alone with your concerns**

At a dozen or so dinner tables over the last year there's always been at least one person who has put me on the spot by asking what I have been writing about.

There's also always been that awkward pause before I would begin my reply, as you might imagine, it really hasn't been an easy subject to bring up at a wedding reception, a neighbour's barbecue or someone's birthday party... but why not?

Once my awkward pauses came to an end I would fire off my rehearsed answer which went something like this: "I'm writing a book to help inspire victims of bullying to come out the other side more positively and to use their experience as a driver to realise their true potential." Usually my initial answer would be a little shorter, but I would always have the chance to elaborate and get the message of my book over as intended.

"It's about... bullying, not your inventions then?"

I would know immediately through questions like this that some of them felt I was entering dangerous waters, maybe being about to come out with some highly personal and unnecessary admissions of weakness on my part. But people would be drawn to the topic and would encourage me to continue. So, there would be more questions, which in fact I didn't then particularly relish answering in these open social situations. However, once the subject was broached, I realised it presented me with a massive opportunity to break open a subject we don't usually share in these types of situations.

# My dilemma

Most people don't know I was bullied, but invariably as soon as I would utter the word "bullied", people's attention would turn to me, they were intrigued and wanted me to continue. Suddenly, everyone would hang on every word I'd say, for many different reasons, I'm sure.

At times when it got heavy I had wanted to say, "Wait for my book to come out because I write better than I talk," but by then it would be too late, the elephant in the room had been allowed to appear and a barrage of questions would be fired my way. It became quite intense, but everyone would sit up and listen.

## Then the real reward

I suppose even at dinner tables and parties it can't always be fun and games, but nonetheless, to me it could be a little bit awkward. **But then the reward would come, big time!**

It would usually happen when the conversation turned to another subject and noisy chatter would fill the room again. At that point, invariably someone would sidle up to me for a private chat. "Oh my God, what you shared happened to me at school," one lady confessed; another told me of her depression due to being bullied at work. These urgent and heartfelt conversations would continue, ignoring all other voices around us. This has happened to me several times, even before the book was published, and I guess I'm hoping it will happen many more times now. This book is for you, all of you who feel that the time has finally come to speak.

I've never been at all surprised by any of these confessions. I see the pain in people's eyes; usually lovely, compassionate, humble people who are laying bare their vulnerability, often after years of keeping it hidden − I see the relief on their faces and the weight lifting from their shoulders as they open up to me.

My experiences of talking to people over the past year has led me to the following conclusion, even if it is based on talking to a random and non-scientific selection of people. Bullying behaviour has been either demonstrated, endured or witnessed by EVERY SINGLE PERSON seated at those tables. It's even the case that some of them have been involved in two or even three of those aspects of bullying. And yet, until I, in my rather awkward way, dared to broach the taboo subject of bullying, I'd never previously heard any of these people ever talk about it before. There's a conspiracy of silence about bullying which needs to be broken down, one dinner table at a time!

Maybe this book will help that process to start; to embolden people to talk about it, to share experiences and find ways to heal the past and fully move on. No one has the right to manipulate anyone of us into their way of thinking, as it can so easily end up as taking unauthorised control, this is what bullies try to do!

All the stories you have read in this book have involved all of us, at some point, submitting to someone else's power and control before then taking it back ourselves. We've all found a way through, no matter how long it has taken or at what point in our lives we hit that low that triggered the response to start the change.

I talked to Ray Dawson about this, whose story is shared in chapter 3 and he encapsulated both our situations so profoundly when he said, "Bullying does not define us. We use it instead to propel ourselves forward and aspire to help others who are or have been victims. We let them know that once you place the blame where it belongs, on the bullies, YOU become a survivor."

I couldn't have said it better myself!

## So, let's look back at what we might take from each story shared...

What is it that has changed Ray Dawson from the boy wanting to roll onto a railway line to end his young life to the person who now wakes up every morning wanting to use every ounce of positivity plus **significant chunks of his own pension** to make dreams come true for the downtrodden and oppressed?

Ray came within a few feet of ending his life as a child but has since successfully stopped others from committing suicide. That part of his life was only touched on in his written story, but it's part of what he does.

Ray sent me a message a few months ago which is so typical of him; this is what he wrote:

"Did you hear about the guy in the job centre where I was volunteering? He made the mistake of saying his dream was to join the circus; he asked why I wasn't laughing like everyone else. One email later, he joined the circus. But that's another story!"

Ray then aimed this compliment at me, which I tried really hard to accept, "We are both blessed with the ability to change lives Graham, isn't that a wonderful thing? Enjoy your evening. Ray."

This incredible gentleman has helped transform hundreds of lives; you only have to hear what others say about him, including dozens of women cruelly abused through domestic violence, the list goes on...

In truth, I couldn't hold a torch to Ray, but no one inspires me quite as much as this gentle soul, and secretly I aspire to be more like him, but please don't tell him.

What happened in Ray's life that changed everything?

Maybe this gives us all a clue...

A few years ago, Ray almost died following a serious illness that plagued him for over a year. He lost so much weight and knew for certain that the next time he closed his eyes that would be it for him. He should have slipped away. Instead, somehow, he miraculously pulled through. Ever since that day he has dedicated his life to "being in the corner of those who feel no one cares about them in society."

How about this situation then? What if Swanny and I had suddenly crossed paths in a pub some 35 years ago? Put it this way, I don't think we'd have hugged like brothers, do you? So, what changed... for us both?

I will come back to what changed for me later, but Swanny? When I met him, he told me he is naturally shy and really has to push himself. I knew this to be true, as glimpses of the lost boy came back when we chatted; I could see and hear him, and I felt his sadness.

A few years ago, Swanny saved one of his best friends from committing suicide. He turned up in the nick of time because of a message he received from God. He started banging on his friend's door before then having to break in. To discover the full story, read his book, it's all in there!

The guy he saved then gave his life to God and has never looked back. Swanny affects lives and saves them, all the time. You've read his story, but there are many more chapters to his life; just ask a few of the hundreds of people who know him now, they will all share a personal story about the man they now hold in high regard.

What is it that makes Sarah and Kay Neumann so positive in the face of such adversity? What lifts them up from the trenches of doom and gloom when most of us might roll over and give up? Could it be their unconditional love for each other, is it the hope they cling onto, that bullying will one day be taken seriously so their pain will end?

I have listened to Sarah's heartache; I've heard her cry and felt her pain.

I know she dreams for a better life for Kay, but it's the compassion she has for those who really hurt them both and continue to do so that blows my mind.

Sarah knows she messes up too; her messages express her frustration and sometimes it comes to the fore. She is naturally passionate and sometimes all too easily reacts to certain situations that affect her or Kay, but that's more than understandable. Money is tight and she struggles, but what she has written to me is one of the most profound and inspiring statements I've ever read, and it's worth highlighting again, it's part of her story in chapter 8:

"I have learned, and also teach Kay, that success is not measured by our bank accounts, the jobs we have, even by the quality of our health, because all that can be taken in a heartbeat. We have had it happen... multiple times. We measure success by our hearts, the way we treat people, and the kindness we do for others. Those are the things that matter in the end. None of the rest of it really does."

And then there is the "medicine" that saved Sarah & Kay's lives, and I am not talking about what a shrink prescribed when Sarah was losing her mind. Her medicine was art, and her wonderful paintings began the healing process. Sarah has passed on this healing medicine to Kay, and now the art is out there to inspire all of us. It's another way to come out of depression, to forget troubles and escape bullying, to think clearly again, to create something beautiful and go again the next day. What might your medicine be?

Thomas Dahlborg was himself bullied at school; it took me a while to get that information out of him. However, this is an important element to the story because, just like Sarah has done for Kay, Thomas has stepped up for his son, Tommy. He has given him, and always will, his unconditional love and support no matter what they face.

Thomas told me he has received more back from son Tommy than he has given him and that's so inspiring: they are a formidable team!

Thomas's strength, I think, is the integrity he demonstrated all through his son's upheavals at the hands of his coaches. He didn't rant and rave at the coach who insinuated that his son, Tommy, was too fat to play for the team, and that he wouldn't play him ever again, even though the coach wouldn't throw him out of the squad. Instead, they calmly and intelligently hatched a plan, and turned what was a potentially devastating moment into eventual triumph. There's a lesson for us all in Thomas and Tommy's story.

Thomas H Dahlborg is a massive influencer in the US healthcare system. He is also a father who has dedicated his life to helping people who struggle. His amazing son Tommy now counsels bully victims. This is the success I am talking about, turning a negative force into a positive opportunity to help save lives!

What brings Taz Thornton from praying for a terminal illness to ravage her body to becoming the UK's #1 Inspirational Breakthrough Speaker? Imagine, this powerhouse lady now stands up in front of hundreds of people on a regular basis telling them how to be positive and awesome! While typing this last chapter I have just experienced three of the most inspiring days I have ever attended: a speaking training course that she and her wife Asha organised. Taz has an authenticity that is relatable to her audience, she had us in the palm of her hand, but more importantly she made it ALL about us. Not every speaker has that special gift.

I wasn't just there to learn how to articulate my story, I wanted to know how Taz rolled too, I wanted to see some evidence of how she turned her life around, and I found it in heaps. Taz spoke about a little about her spiritual learning based on the shamanic path. She talked about life balance and being able to peel away the masks we've learned to create and connect with the authentic self. The point is, without going into more detail, it was clear that her spiritual teachings have been at the centre of her own personal healing.

Taz is hugely intelligent and teaches her audience so much, bringing out emotion and often tears from individuals who swore before entering the room they wouldn't allow it, including me. Her words are soothing and relatable and she connects with each of those who make the effort to sit before her, she shows that level of respect.

Taz has shared the incredible abuse she has experienced in her life, and even though she glosses over some areas of pain that have been unbearable, the hurt she has felt isn't lost on us; instead, it's like she's speaking about another person.

That's how Taz sees it all; she's been hurt badly but there is no way she is letting this affect her life negatively, quite the opposite. Taz reaches out to all types of audiences that are seeking motivation. Most particularly, if you are part of an organisation that deals with mental health issues, I strongly recommend that you contact Taz, as you will be in safe hands. You can find her details at tazthornton.com.

How about Asha, the lady with the beautiful smile and sparkling eyes? She's the other half of the dynamic duo. Taz & Asha are an amazing partnership and married couple. I chatted to Asha at the venue where we conducted our speaker training. Asha also got up and spoke about the PR strategies and marketing required to get speaking gigs. She presented this wearing her journalist hat and was wonderfully engaging and insightful.

Asha is the sort of person that gives you a hug and even shares a tear with you when it's needed. She has this soothing karma about her which is a joy to experience.

I was left thinking about her personal pain in dealing with those family issues based around her sexuality. How has she handled her past traumas? I think it is similar to Taz, with the shamanic teachings being a big part of it.

I noticed, through the smile of love and admiration Asha displayed on her face every time Taz stood up to speak, how much she loved her, and that this was equally reciprocated too. There's something about this couple, they feed off each other.

The most important factor for me in writing this book has been to bring more awareness to the issues surrounding bullying. I have felt so privileged to have had an opportunity to receive such amazing support from everyone who has given an account of those hugely difficult parts of their life in my book.

It's great to see in each story how people have used painful parts of their lives to not only rebuild, but to go on to have a positive effect on so many others.

The being bullied moments in my life could be described as just one or two pages of my whole life, but if you ripped them out you might just as well rip the others out too. I have come to realise that those pages have such a bearing on the rest of my life's chapters. Without those pages, would I have been the joker who tried to compensate my personality to try and reinvent myself in a way I (falsely) thought would make people like me? I doubt it. Would I have ended up in hospital following an almost fatal car accident? I don't know. Would I have become a successful inventor and businessman? I honestly don't think I would. The bullying experiences, without a shred of doubt, instilled in me the desire and drive to do well in the business world.

Maybe if I had been more outgoing and confident in various areas of my life, my beautiful wife Sue wouldn't have married me. The list of what–ifs goes on and on.

Those pages didn't mean that every chapter in my life needed to be poisoned too. They just forced me into a position to choose whether I would move forward and use what had happened positively or negatively. Or, to put it another way, whether I would use those painful experiences as a springboard to aspire to live a life I wanted instead of the life my bullies would have chosen for me.

> **66 Bullying is a horrible thing. 99**
> **It sticks with you forever.**
> **It poisons you.**
> **But only if you let it.**
>
> Heather Brewer

Maybe my success as an inventor has been driven by me wanting to make something of myself, to prove to Graham Harris that I wasn't the joker or no-hoper I thought bullies and others took me for. In truth, I didn't need to think this; my wife loved me just as much when we struggled to rub two pennies together.

This doesn't mean that those of us who are held back in some way through the effects of bullying shouldn't strive to own our own business or strive for the best career, or be the best mother, father, sister, brother, neighbour or human being we can be. I think that having a goal to live your own life the way you want to is amazing enough, and I hope my book helps you to do this.

The tough part for me in writing this book, and I know others who have contributed their stories have felt the same, was going back over what happened all over again.

In my case, once again to run away from the cousins and dozens of others that taunted and beat me. To live through my shame of hitting the big guy who bullied me at work, or to cry again when my parents gathered outside the operating theatre not knowing whether their son was dead or alive.

Writing this book has both hurt and healed me, but I don't have any regrets!

I own my own dreams and have the freedom to pursue them as I wish, no matter how big or small. I have retained my own character traits; I resisted having them beaten out of me. I have been Bullied Back To Life!

# What about you?

And that's it, in a nutshell. I have achieved so much, I have won back my self-confidence and my freedom to choose my own path, that's my real success... or is it? I think my real success, moving forward from this point on, is in how I use my story and my knowledge from this book to help other victims.

What about **YOU?** Regardless of whether you were bullied, bullying is not unknown to you. You have at the very least seen it happen, read about it or watched it on TV. It's all around us, in all our lives, every day, if you care to look.

## Change Starts With Us

I am not asking you to be hyper-sensitive or to go on some crusade. It's about each of us taking some personal responsibility for our own thoughts and actions. I just want people to be more aware of how others receive our words and perceive our actions, my own and yours.

We don't always know what others are going through; they are sometimes too proud to tell us. Think about it this way: a little "innocent" comment can end up like a poison arrow that pierces someone else's heart. A "kind piece of advice" to a friend might make you feel better, but it might shatter someone else's confidence.

I met a beautiful, amazing lady at a business seminar who told me and a few others that it took her months to pluck up courage to go outside because of her weight and anxiety issues. No sooner had she ventured out than she heard some guy ask his friend if he'd "seen the sight of THAT! walking by?"

This lady was faced with a choice – do her best to ignore the comment or face it head-on. She decided to confront the guy, looked him squarely in the face and told him she thought he had beautiful eyes! He shamefully looked down and then apologised. As she carried on walking to the shops, she turned back to see his wife slap him around the head! That was one of the most inspiring stories I have heard in how quickly and effectively we can hand back to a bully their shame! If you had met this lady and heard her story you would know how difficult it was for her to go through that experience, as she cried when telling it.

**To some friends and dinner guests at those tables, NO, I didn't need to write this book, I mean who really wants to admit to being bullied anyway?**

Actually, I do, and so do all the super-talented and ultra-positive people who have shared their stories so graciously: Ray, Taz, Asha, Swanny, Sarah and Kay, Thomas and Tommy, Linda and Casey-Jane.

SO, why attract attention to ourselves by sharing something so personal as being bullied and being perceived as weak? It's simple: we know there is NO SHAME attached to it, and if our bullies ever thought they left us with their shame, having reached these final few sentences in my book, you will know that they have failed miserably!

We are most definitely not ashamed; in fact we all feel hugely honoured to be able to share our stories in order to highlight the fact that acts of bullying are everywhere and that we don't have to carry the weight of our trauma and heartbreak for the rest of our lives. **And much more importantly, if you're in that place now, neither should you!**

Bullied Back to Life

# Acknowledgements

Most authors will know of the sacrifices that others make while they write, particularly by those closest to them who step aside to let them pour those words onto the pages. My wife, Sue, has put up with my absence of mind if not physical presence while I've put in the hours and burnt the midnight oil, on and off, for a whole year, to produce this book. Sue, from the bottom of my heart, thank you for your support, you know how important it has been for me to complete this book, and I know I have pushed things a bit too far at times. I love you so much!

To Sophie, our daughter, son-in-law Adam and our wonderful grandson Harrison, and to Jack, our son and his girlfriend Charlie Anne, you all mean the world to me. Your love, support and patience hasn't gone unnoticed, while I have drifted in and out of conversations. I am back on planet Earth now!

To Ray, Taz, Asha, Swanny, Thomas, Tommy, Sarah and Kay: without your incredible stories and your willingness to share them, there simply would be no book. You guys are all amazing and you will help to mend so many broken hearts through your brave contribution to this project, I have come to love and respect you all!

To Linda, Casey-Jane and the wonderful BulliesOut team, I am so privileged to be one of your volunteers and to have an opportunity to help in some small way by donating the proceeds of the sales of this book to your incredible charity! You can find out more about their great work at BulliesOut.com.

And last but by no means least to two people who have helped me to get this book to the standard I could never have envisaged...

Mark Beaumont-Thomas (Lexicon Marketing), my incredible editor, I owe you a deep debt of gratitude. Your dedication, amazing work ethic and talent helped make this book possible. Mark, your contribution went beyond the remit as you tirelessly put in the research and helped shape this book into something I am so proud of. Thank you, Mark for all those unsociable hours you gave up and for the passion you poured into my book, you truly have been a pleasure to work with.

I also would like to extend my thanks to Sam Pearce, owner of Swatt Books, who has made the process of self-publishing my book seem incredibly easy, even though I know it has been anything but. You have been so organised, extremely professional and have taken away all the headaches I would have encountered had your company not been highly recommended to me.

Lightning Source UK Ltd.
Milton Keynes UK
UKHW020630080120
356583UK00013B/1044/P